About the Author

Theolyn Cortens has channelled celestial messages for over thirty years and has a Master's degree from the University of Wales, based on her angel research. She is a qualified adult education teacher and runs workshops and diploma courses in developing spiritual awareness through contact with angels. She is also the author of *Living with Angels, Working with your Guardian Angel* and *Working with Archangels* for Piatkus.

Why you should read this book

Do you know what it is like to be truly whole, at one with your Divine Soul and with the Universal Creative Intelligence that creates and sustains you?

It is to know the true power of Love and its infinite capacity to heal all discord, all suffering, all wounds. It is to be in love with this Love. It is to know and feel this Love as It moves in every cell of your physical body, with every beat of your heart, with every breath you take. This Love allows you to be so small the fairies can whisper in your ear, so tall you can call to eagles in the mountaintops. The power of this Love takes you deep into the heart of Fire, high through the Air that wraps our planet, plunges you through Water to the ocean bed, and stands you as a giant, stretching your feet across the Earth.

Each of us has a Guardian, a guiding spirit, an Angel, who is calling to us from a quiet, still place inside – a place we seldom experience, a place that will surprise us every time we visit. Your Guardian Angel is calling you. You need to get to know your Guardian – your Guardian Angel needs you, because love is not true Love until two become One.

Theolyn Cortens, Newcastle Emlyn, April 2010

Your Guardian Angel Needs You!

Theolyn Cortens

piatkus

PIATKUS

First published in Great Britain in 2011 by Piatkus

Copyright © 2011 Theolyn Cortens

A CIP catalogue record for this book
is available from the British Library.

ISBN 978-0-7499-5326-3

Typeset in Palatino by M Rules
Printed and bound in Great Britain by
MPG Books, Bodmin, Cornwall

Papers used by Piatkus are natural, renewable and
recyclable products sourced from well-managed forests and certified
in accordance with the rules of the Forest Stewardship Council.

Mixed Sources
Product group from well-managed
forests and other controlled sources
www.fsc.org   Cert no. SGS-COC-004081
© 1996 Forest Stewardship Council
FSC

Piatkus
An imprint of
Little, Brown Book Group
100 Victoria Embankment
London EC4Y 0DY

An Hachette UK Company
www.hachette.co.uk

www.piatkus.co.uk

For Rover, with unconditional love

Contents

Acknowledgements

Thank you to . . .

. . . my dear husband, Will, for his exhaustive copy-editing, proof-reading and stories, and for helping me through the challenge of talking to camera.

Tam and Sean, for magical space at Cwmwenallt.

Paddy and Louis for their open-hearted welcome to Wales.

SoulSchool teachers Denise Vowles, Valentia Lythrin and Julie Ransley, for their commitment to SoulSchool over the years.

Shefa practitioners everywhere, with a special 'thank you' to the Norwegian gang: Iwona, Lis, Kari, Reidun, Christine, Sissel D. and Sissel N., and to Nina at Energica for making the Norwegian connection possible.

Peter and Grethe for their generous hospitality in Oslo.

Chrissie Astell and Kathleen Pepper for their Guardian Angel stories.

All the many students around the world who contributed to the success of the *Your Guardian Angel Needs You!* eClasses and for your stories, especially Veronique, Leena, Nina, Maddy, Sue and Siri.

Eric Gladwin for his encouragement and his amazing dedication – ninety-five and still totally committed to spreading the word.

My cheerleaders in the invisible realms.

A note about visualisations

In order to make the best use of the creative visualisations in this book, you need to be able to close your eyes and listen to someone's voice leading you on an inner journey. You can record this for yourself, allowing short silences where indicated in the text, or you can buy pre-recorded visualisations as MP3 downloads from my website, *www.yourguardianangelneedsyou.co.uk* to play on your computer or MP3 player. Recorded versions of the visualisations are also available on a CD which can be purchased from the website.

Give yourself plenty of time either side of your visualisations. Before starting, make sure you have created a suitably peaceful space where you won't be interrupted; make it physically comfortable and add any items you feel will give you a sense of sacred purpose, such as candles, incense, crystals and so on. Sitting upright on a chair or settee is usually best. Some people prefer to lie down, but this may encourage you to go to sleep.

After your visualisation, make sure you are well grounded. Drink a glass of water, do some simple stretches, perhaps even stamp on the ground (for more information on this see page 60). Some of the visualisations encourage you to look at old issues in your life, so if you are aware of any serious early life traumas, such as childhood abuse, I advise you to talk to a therapist or counsellor before using them. They could be very helpful for you, but you may need additional support.

Using visualisations is quite safe for people in sound psychological health. If you suffer from any serious mental-health problems, however, please consult your therapeutic or medical adviser before undertaking the visualisations in this book.

Introduction

The minute I heard my first love story
I started looking for you, not knowing
  how blind that was.
Lovers don't finally meet somewhere.
They're in each other all along.

RUMI

In 2005, I wrote a book called *Working with your Guardian Angel*, a twelve-week course designed to help you build a relationship with your Guardian Angel and discover your life's purpose. In the years that have passed since that book started to wing its way around the world, I have been teaching lots of people to get in touch with their Guardian Angel – their divine mentor and Soul coach. But most of us have a long way to go before we can reach our potential and become fully realised as complete beings, who are one hundred per cent divine and one hundred per cent human. The journey towards experiencing life from this realisation, which would be pure joy, free of anxiety and pain, can be an up-and-down, round-and-round pathway and we need plenty of reassurance along the way.

Why your Guardian Angel needs you

When the title *Your Guardian Angel Needs You!* arrived in my mind during a meditation, I asked why the Guardian Angels want help from us. We tend to think that it is the Angels' task to look after us – we need them, not the other way around. The answer was very clear and had an urgent quality: all the Guardian Angels need us to turn towards them in order to reconnect with our divine birthright. Then, the collective future of humanity will be bright and beautiful, our planet will flourish and we, as well as all our descendants, will enjoy abundance, joy and love.

Your Guardian Angel is not just a protective guide, watching over you as you travel along the unpredictable road of life, nor simply your spiritual voice of conscience. Your Guardian is your divinity, your *daimon*, your *genius*, calling you to step into the beautiful template created by your Soul. You are being summoned to stretch beyond your self-imposed limitations to become something greater than you have imagined; an amazing, brilliant person, shining in the world as a beacon of light. The divine call is urgent – for if not now, when?

Your Guardian is your mentor and teacher, who opens the gateways to celestial realms, those invisible resources in our consciousness where we discover our true nature as cosmic beings, capable of so much more than we normally expect of ourselves. Many of the challenges we meet in life have been set up by our Guardian Angel, who will comfort us when times are hard but, if we are truly committed to spiritual development, will also test us until we hear the wake-up call and take action.

We are all being called

Spiritual expansion is essential at this time in history. Development of mystical or cosmic consciousness is no longer only for the reclusive yogi or monk and many ordinary people are realising that the challenges in their material lives signal a necessity to address their spiritual needs. There are numerous signs and portents – social, economic, ecological and cosmological – telling us that our survival demands a quantum leap into a new way of being. Humanity is driving itself towards a collective shift in consciousness and this dramatic turnaround needs to happen very soon. You too can contribute to this change by committing to your own spiritual development.

The potential for this enhanced consciousness is hard-wired into your system already, but you have to allow the divine part of your being to grow and flourish. It is your Guardian Angel who summons you to stretch your spiritual limbs and blossom, bringing forth fruit that you can be proud of. The new world that beckons will be filled with people who are radiant and confident, fully aware of their divine nature, and your Guardian Angel will support you every step of the way, if you are committed to that bright future. Are you ready to step into this new way of living?

My journey with the Angels

I have been talking to invisible people for over thirty years! Perhaps certain medical professionals would find a label for me, but my answer to them would be that my conversations with angels and other spiritual beings have brought great joy and delight into my life and haven't interfered with me having meaningful relationships with other people. Nor have these unusual habits of mine stopped me from living a happy life. In fact, quite the opposite, my invisible helpers have allowed me to be in the world, experiencing many ups and downs, some of which have been very dramatic, without losing my sense of humour. I want to encourage you to engage in these inner dialogues so that you can also access inner wisdom, which can help you deal with everyday issues.

Spiritual curiosity and bright visions

The only reason I have had some very beautiful experiences and have found myself writing books to help other people is because I have always wanted know the how, the what and the why of being alive. Like Rudyard Kipling's elephant child, I suffer from 'satiable curtiosity' (that is, insatiable curiosity) – and, like the elephant, I have often found my nosiness puts me out of favour with other folk. But when the curious elephant was severely tested by the crocodile, his nose, which was originally very short and stubby like an old boot, grew longer and longer and he found the end result very useful. So curiosity is rewarded with a new, more exciting way of being. (You really must read this story if you don't already know it! (See Recommended books, p. 223.)

When I was small, my family had no television and lived in an isolated rural area with few social opportunities, so I often read books that belonged to the grown-ups. We were not religious, but I was able to find out about a variety of faiths and, when I was only fourteen, I joined the Buddhist Society. I was only a postal member, so I couldn't go to meditation groups until we all moved to London when I was sixteen. Over the years I read about spirituality and techniques for raising consciousness that open the mind to different dimensions. I also studied astrology. In the early 1970s I learned Transcendental Meditation; this was the trigger for a powerful spiritual opening and I experienced several exquisite moments being filled with light from head to toe. One very special 'visitation' of light happened one afternoon at the summer solstice, after I had been ill in bed for a couple of weeks. Although I didn't see a figure with wings, I did wonder whether it was an Angel that had called on me, but there didn't seem to be a 'message' so I puzzled about its meaning.

After the light from my 'visitor' had closed down, I found my mind was being filled with so much otherworldly information that it was all too much for me to assimilate. At the time, I was a single mum with two daughters at school and I was trying hard to create a stable life for us. I concentrated on organising everyday matters and tried to forget about Heaven! Then I was blessed by meeting Will. We married and had two more daughters, so I shifted my attention to the practical and put my spiritual interests mostly to the back of my mental cupboard. But once the door to other dimensions has been opened, there will always be a calling and an opening. We cannot turn away from this destiny: our Soul is always yearning for the hidden ingredient that our Guardian has in safe-keeping. Just as a cake does not rise without baking soda, our lives will be flat and meaningless if we do not activate the divinity we all carry within.

How I discovered my guides

By the early 1980s, Will and I had moved to Somerset, so we could be near Glastonbury, and most of my time was occupied with earning a living and being a parent. But I often found myself scribbling poetry on scraps of paper – words that seemed to come from 'somewhere else'. I took up meditating again and sometimes found myself having inner conversations with wise mentors. One of my visitors was an old man with a long white beard and twinkling eyes. I asked him if he was the Maharishi – after all, I had learned his system of meditation – but the old man told me he was Pythagoras. All I knew about this famous Greek teacher was what I had learned in geometry lessons about his work on right-angled triangles! I did some research and discovered he had been an esoteric teacher who had an amazing reputation as a healer and was reputed to levitate. He advised me to study Western philosophy, and I decided to enrol on a course with the Open University. I had already studied Eastern philosophies, so I found this new interest stimulating and balancing. We could say that Eastern thought is more 'right-brained' and Western thought more 'left-brained' – learning about both allowed me to gain a new perspective, and to value both my intuitive and my rational abilities. Another visitor in my meditations was a beautiful lady who called herself Astarte. She was dressed in a Greek-style gown and carried a staff, surmounted by a large pearl. Twisting around the staff was a snake. She told me these symbols represented Wisdom and that I should dedicate myself to its pursuit.

These inner visions were very powerful. They seemed to arise out of nowhere and I began to trust that my meditations could reveal all kinds of helpful spiritual insights, so I was not entirely surprised when an Archangel revealed himself to me.

How I learned to talk to Archangels

We were living in a tiny village called Pedwell. From our windows we could see an amazing hill topped by seven pine trees in a circle. I often went for a walk along the track that ran beside the foot of the hill, pushing our small daughter in her pram. One day I felt a very strange sensation, as though the atmosphere was filled with a huge presence. Everything seemed very still and I felt as though I needed to stop breathing and stay connected to something much, much larger than myself. I didn't see or hear anything, but had the impression that there was someone filling the air around me with intense energy. The moment passed and I returned home, wondering whether I had come into contact with a spirit who lived in the hill, perhaps a *deva*, who was responsible for the surrounding landscape.

A few days later, during my meditation, I saw on my inner 'cinema screen' a beautiful Angel, walking in sandalled feet through a landscape, just like the one outside the house. He was amazingly tall and, with his shining feathered wings and glowing halo, he seemed to fill the sky. In one hand he carried an olive branch, in the other a blue crystal. At his feet danced a small lamb and in the distance beyond I could see a hill, like the one at Pedwell. At the top was a building that seemed to be made of glass, shining light beams across the surrounding countryside. Afterwards I attempted to paint a picture of this Angel, but, even though I had been to art school, my attempts to paint him were not very satisfactory. As William Blake said, 'Who can paint an Angel?'

At this time there were no New Age Angel books around, but not long afterwards I found an art book about Angels and, when I opened the first page, there was a clue to my Angel's identity. A large black-and-white picture from the Renaissance showed an old man with a diagram labelled in Hebrew. This, I learned, was the Tree of Life, which describes the way Divine Energy flows through Creation in repeating patterns, based on pathways and reservoirs. At each reservoir, sometimes called Gates of Light, an Archangel stands guard. Some names of these Archangels were familiar to me – Michael and Gabriel were mentioned – but one was called Sandalphon and I immediately thought of the sandals I had noticed my Angel visitor wearing. The reservoirs on the Tree of Life are called *sefirot* in Hebrew, a word that is connected to 'sapphire' – my Angel had been carrying a blue crystal. I was sure I had been guided to read this book and from that moment my journey with the Archangels of the Tree of Life began.

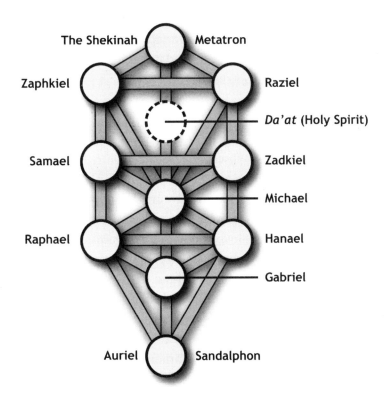

The Archangels of the Tree of Life

Over many months, during meditation, I spent time asking to meet the other Archangels. I imagined the Tree of Life as a tall building with a lift. In my mind I would go into the lift and ask to reach another level, giving the name of the Archangel I wanted to meet. I would visualise the doors sliding open and hope to see the

Archangel of my choice. Sometimes I had no luck at all! Sometimes I would see something that I felt was not a 'true' image. For example, when I asked to meet Gabriel, the images that came to me were obviously based on Christmas cards or paintings I had seen. I always knew when a vision was 'true' because it presented itself with great intensity and colour, and surrounded me with energy, rather than being static.

I recorded my meetings and experiences in a notebook, and eventually wrote my first book, *Discovering Angels,* in 1989. The public interest in Angels had not started to blossom, so in 1992 I published the book myself. I circulated it among people I knew and started giving talks and workshops.

Research into spiritual experiences

My experiences led me to discover a research centre that specialised in collecting and analysing spiritual experiences. The Alister Hardy Research Centre had been founded by an Oxford professor in 1969 and, while Will was designing books for Oxford University Press in the early 1990s, I became involved with the organisation. My interest was to find out more about the kind of experiences I had been having. I also wanted to discover how many other people have them as well. I later signed up for a Master's degree, studying the psychological aspects of spirituality, poetry and mysticism, the way culture affects people's experiences and whether human beings the world over have experiences in common. My dissertation was all about Angels! I researched the long history of humanity's relationship with the angelic kingdoms, from the earliest stories that go back several thousands of years to the present day.

My passion to help you discover your divine potential

Alongside my academic research, I always kept up my meditation. As Pythagoras had advised me, I was using and developing both my rational and my intuitive faculties. I also began to teach more people, organising home-study courses and sending out CDs so that people could experience the Archangels for themselves. I eventually found a publisher who wanted books about Angels and my titles have since been translated into many languages.

My aim is to help you open up your heart and mind to the glory of the divine kingdoms. I want you to transform yourself into a powerful, compassionate, wise person – the amazing, glorious person you could be, if you were to step out of the old and into the new. My passionate and urgent plea is that you should be totally committed to your own highest possibility.

Your Guardian Angel needs your unswerving dedication and the future of humanity depends on us all focusing on a new vision – a vision of Heaven on Earth.

PART ONE

Finding Your Guardian Angel

1

Introducing Your Guardian Angel

Happy those early days, when I
Shin'd in my angel-infancy …
When yet I had not walked above
A mile or two from my first love,
And looking back – at that short space –
Could see a glimpse of his bright face.

HENRY VAUGHAN

Guardian Angels from early times

We know from many stories in ancient texts that the idea of a guardian or guiding spirit has been around for thousands of years. The Assyrians, who lived in the Middle East from around 3000 BCE, believed that good genii, called *shedu* or *lamassu*, watched over individuals, defending them against evil powers and carrying their prayers to the gods. These genii were invisible, but always present, following human beings in their everyday lives, whether they were walking in the streets or fighting in battles. The Assyrians had a saying, 'He who has no god when he walks in the street wears a headache like a garment.' I thought this was a great idea and it is very true – if we do not acknowledge the support of our Guardian we will have headaches, because it is impossible to make all our decisions and choices without referring to the higher purpose behind our everyday life.

The Greek playwright, Menander of Athens, who lived about three hundred years before Jesus, said: 'Beside each man who is born on Earth, a Guardian Angel takes his stand to guide him through life's mysteries.'

The Greek word for our guiding spirit was *daimon*, not to be confused with 'demon'! The word has become popular with a wider audience through Philip Pullman's *His Dark Materials* trilogy, in which everyone has a *daimon*, visible to other people, in the shape of a creature of some kind, such as a monkey or a weasel. The children's *daimons* could change shape because they hadn't matured into a fixed way of being.

The famous philosopher Plato describes how, before conception, our Soul has the ability to choose its future life and calls on a *daimon* to be a constant advisor and supporter. The three Moirae, or Fates, who are daughters of Night, watch over this process. Clotho (the spinner) spins the thread of life from her distaff on to a spindle; Lachesis (the drawing of lots) measures this thread with her measuring rod and Atropos (the inevitable) cuts the thread. In this way, the pattern and length of our life is formulated, as though we have made a contract, which will have to be honoured, however much free will we may think we have. In this myth, the Moirae have to submit to the authority of Zeus, who commands them to see that the natural order of things is respected. This means there is an overarching plan for humanity as a whole – one that governs our smaller lives.

Plato goes on to describe how, as we descend into the living human world, we forget this contract and have to rediscover our choices. In his poem, 'Intimations of Immortality', Wordsworth says the same thing:

Our birth is but a sleep and a forgetting:
The Soul that rises with us, our life's star,
Has had elsewhere its setting
And cometh from afar ...
Trailing clouds of glory do we come
From God who is our home ...

A similar idea can be found in West Africa. People belonging to the Yoruba tradition, believe humans have made a pre-birth contract with Olorun (God) and when they are born, all the details of this contract are hidden in the *ori-inu* – or 'inner head'. During their lives they have to work hard to remember their original plan. One technique for remembering this contract involves what we would call art therapy. The seeker creates a *ju-ju*, a shrine dedicated to the inner head. The *ju-ju* provides an image that can be 'read' and awakens the memory of the pre-birth choices.

The Romans called the guiding spirit our *genius*. We tend to use this word for people who are exceptionally gifted, but the original meaning confirms that *everyone* has one. Perhaps the people we label geniuses are those who listen to their inner voice and carry through their pre-birth contracts. But all human beings have the same capacity to be extraordinary and our Guardian Angels will support those who focus on living with true commitment to their amazing possibilities.

In the Christian tradition, Guardian Angels were appointed to make sure we all behaved ourselves. The early Church Fathers debated whether a person who was not baptised would have a Guardian Angel. Eventually they decided everyone must have one, otherwise there would be no heavenly helper on hand, encouraging people to become Christians! St Basil said that everyone would have 'an Angel who directs his life', but thought that mortal sin would lead the Guardian to abandon his post. St Thomas Aquinas thought that no one could ever be abandoned. Much later, the Roman Catholic Church decided that everyone, however good or bad, and regardless of their religion, must have a Guardian Angel because it was the job of these Guardians to bring everyone into the Catholic fold. The Church also suggested that the celestial status of the Guardian Angel would reflect the earthly status of the human: bishops and priests obviously had more dignified and grander Guardians than the rest of us! Some people I meet on my travels say their Guardian Angel is one of the great Archangels and others seem disappointed when their Guardian says their name is Tom. But we have to accept the 'ordinary' and the 'grand' on equal terms – God made both the wren and the peacock, after all.

In Jewish mysticism, a *maggid* is a kind of personal spirit that sends messages from heaven and many old kabbalists speak of a powerful impulse to communicate words that seem to come from this higher power. The sixteenth-century kabbalist, Joseph Caro, described nightly visits from his *maggid*, who assured him of constant access to wisdom:

> The voice of my beloved began to knock on my mouth, saying: 'Although you imagined I had forsaken you and left you, do not think I will leave you before I have fulfilled my promise not to withhold good from your mouth ...'

I think our Guardian Angel *is* our 'beloved', our other half. No wonder the Guardian Angels need us just as much as we need them, otherwise how can the love of the Divine be expressed in the world?

Why doesn't our Guardian Angel always rescue us?

Sometimes people feel they have been abandoned or not protected during times of difficulty. There are three good reasons why an Angel might allow what appears to be a negative course to unfold: trial, foresight or karma:

❖ **Tests or trials** These have a spiritual purpose – to help you discover your strengths and weaknesses, so that you can set about growing and maturing, hopefully to become a wiser person. If we sit around wondering 'Why me?', then we fail the test. We need to accept our tests with good grace, knowing that all humans, rich and poor, whatever gender or race, are all being tested to one degree or another.

❖ **Foresight** This is the underlying meaning behind some difficulties. Maybe your Guardian Angel can see you beginning to drift off your path, perhaps making a bad choice, and will attempt to nudge you in a different direction. You might have signed up for a college course on the basis that it would be a good career move leading to a reliable income, but your Guardian Angel knows you have arrived on this planet to do something more meaningful. Then you trip up and break a leg and end up in bed for several weeks, with plenty of time to contemplate your future and perhaps change your plans.

❖ **Karma** This is the law of cause and effect. Everything we do has a result at one level or another. We may not observe this immediately, but eventually we reap what we sow. If we sow flower seeds, we will have a pretty garden. Think of the flower seeds as your positive thoughts and actions, which lead to beautiful results. When we sow negative actions or thoughts, we are scattering seeds for weeds and brambles, the kinds of plants that strangle our heartfelt desires. So negative events, which we might perceive as having no rhyme or reason, can be the result of a backlog of difficult karma. We may not be able to see the bigger picture or how far back the original cause might have been, but we can trust that if we shift the negative karma out of the way, our path will be cleared of weeds and we will be able to move ahead with a lighter heart.

My philosophy is to accept all our trials as part of the process of growing. Complaining only plants more negative seeds, so we might as well 'grow up and get on with it' – or 'GUAGOWI', as we say in our household.

Your higher self, guides and Guardian Angels

I am often asked whether your Guardian Angel is the same as either your higher self or your guides.

Your 'higher self' is exactly what it says; it is a higher aspect of your everyday self, which is your interface with the world. Your 'self' and your body are extensions of your Soul. Imagine a series of layers, linked together like a chain, in which your everyday self links to your higher self and your higher self to your Soul. Your Guardian Angel is a messenger between your Soul and your higher self, which in turn calls your everyday self to attend to divine wisdom.

Your guides can be all sorts of characters, including animals – sometimes called 'power animals'. Human guides have lived life on Earth before you and can provide practical guidance when there are worldly decisions to make. Your Guardian Angel may call you to the highest possibility that your Soul requires, but sometimes you cannot see how you can measure up to this demand. You may feel it would not be practical, for example, to give up your steady job in order to spend more time playing music, which is your Soul's call-ing. Perhaps you have only just realised what your real purpose is, but there are lots of obstacles in the way. Apart from asking for guidance from your Guardian Angel, you can ask for help from a spiritual guide. Just as you might want some good advice from a friend or colleague, you are able to summon help from all kinds of celestial beings, power animals, your ancestors, or people who had expertise in your subject when they were alive. A budding musician might ask for advice from famous musician. I will be sharing more information about inner guidance in Chapter 14.

The entrepreneur Napoleon Hill (1883–1970) wrote *Think and Grow Rich*, a popular book in which he suggested that people could become more successful if they gathered together a 'mastermind' team of likeminded businessmen (see Recommended books, p. 223). But, he said, these people didn't necessarily have to be living. He described how he would visualise a 'board meeting' to which he would invite several famous dead Americans, including presidents.

He asked them to be his guides as he developed his business, tackling the everyday problems that occur in all kinds of human endeavour, because he knew that these great men had probably dealt with the same kinds of problems in their own lifetimes.

Guides can turn up spontaneously, as Pythagoras did for me. I hadn't even thought of asking for a guide. Your own ancestors or recently deceased relatives can appear as your guides. One thing is very clear to me, however: that while guides can come and go (whether appearing spontaneously or answering your call for help) your Guardian Angel is the same for ever. Although Plato describes how the Soul has chosen its *daimon* immediately before conception, my impression is that the same Guardian Angel watches over us from our first incarnation. I think our Guardian continues to be with us during the periods in between our human lives, when we are learning more as discarnated Souls, or if we experience lives that are not human, perhaps on another planet. Earth has been called 'the only planet of choice', and a 'vale of soul-making', so most of us will spend many incarnations here, learning the lessons that are only available to us as humans, because we have free will. For me, this way of thinking about my Guardian Angel gives me a sense of continuity and constancy that makes me feel supported, not just for a few decades, but over many possible lifetimes behind me and ahead of me.

Our spiritual mentor, teacher and beloved

For Christians, the Guardian Angel was a moral teacher, encouraging people to abide by the religious doctrines of the Church. Personally, I prefer the earlier kind of Guardians, who existed to support life choices, whether these conformed to Christian doctrine or other opinions of any kind. We invariably notice that the geniuses of this world overturn conventional thinking, because they 'march to a different beat'. This musical metaphor is very helpful when thinking about your own Guardian Angel. If we imagine that each of us is playing a musical phrase in the symphony of human experience, there is an impulse to create harmony; but how dull it would be if we all played the same tune on the same instrument.

Your Guardian Angel is a mentor, constantly calling you to return to the Divine Source of your being. This Angel may feel more masculine for women and more feminine for men, but Angels do not have any gender and their names are mostly only to help us develop a sense of intimacy with them. When you meet your Guardian Angel and ask for a name, this could be something like 'Jack' or 'Mary', which may seem a bit prosaic. But you can always politely say you would prefer to choose another name – they are very amenable! You may not receive a name at all, in which case you should feel quite free to find one that seems suitable.

As a mentor, your Guardian's task is to keep pulling the thread that reminds you of your origins. G. K. Chesterton, in one of his famous Father Brown stories, wrote that God keeps us all on a fishing line, with an unseen hook and an invisible line which allows us to wander to the ends of the world. But God has only to twitch the thread in order to bring us back. We need to remember that although we have free will, there is a Divine Source on which we depend – and we need to respect it. When we turn inwards during meditation and allow ourselves to drink in the spiritual refreshment that is freely available, we open our hearts to the love and grace of the Divine Source. Then we are less likely to suffer anxiety or encounter negative events in our daily lives. We are also more likely to follow the thread of our divine contract, the destiny we chose before we were born.

Our Guardian is also a teacher, finding opportunities for us to glean spiritual wisdom, either by offering encouragement or by chastising us when we stray. The more we resist the lessons, the tougher they can seem, until something suddenly goes 'click' and we gain a clear perspective. Teaching situations can include just happening to come across a particular book in a second-hand shop, a book that changes the way you look at the world. Or perhaps being called away to look after a sick relative when your workload is overwhelming – you resent having to spend time away, but from a distance you see what you are doing to yourself, something you might not have realised if you had kept going to the office.

But the most beautiful role for our Guardian is as our 'Beloved', who offers us love without conditions and allows us to love in return, giving as much as we are able. The more we turn to this love, the greater will be our capacity to receive and give love. All the exercises and visualisations in this book are designed to help you open your heart to the love of your Guardian Angel, so that you always feel the presence of your own Beloved.

I have known Chrissie Astell for many years. She is a well-known teacher, who has written several books about Angels. This is her own description of an amazing experience she had when she was feeling desperate actually to see an Angel.

CHRISSIE'S STORY

One afternoon, around teatime, I had finished my shift at the nursing home and was enjoying reading one of my Angel books. As I read some of the words aloud, invoking the Archangels Raphael, Uriel, Michael and Gabriel for healing the planet Earth, I was suddenly overwhelmed with emotion. As tears softly ran down my face, I called out in frustration to the heavens: 'I have dedicated the rest of my life in service to you, why can I not see you? Please, Angels, let me see you!'

I looked up, out of the window. Instantly, there was a dazzling bright light in front of me. It came shining through the patio windows, immediately in front of my balcony. I stood up and walked to the window. In the sky, as clear as a photograph, was a huge white Angel. I stared. I could hardly believe my eyes. The light formed an even brighter, pure white angelic form. I wanted to see the face, as I so often see faces in my meditations, particularly when I'm giving healing. Instead of features, the face was the brightest golden light, as bright as the sun, and I couldn't look into it.

I sensed a strong masculine presence, which surprised me. I was even more amazed to see two pairs of wings. I would never have imagined two pairs! One huge pair reached high and pointed upwards into the sky, with the other curved and folded behind 'his' back. I stared at 'his' feet and toes, softly covered by the fabric of a gown, which swayed gently in the air. Then, as I stood and connected with this beautiful and majestic being, I absolutely knew in my heart that I recognised him and that he knew me too.

The feeling of love I experienced that day I have never felt before or since – it can't even be adequately described. I have never found the right words and I guess that is what the mystics call 'ineffable'. Every cell in my body, mind and Soul felt totally loved and in love. All I could do was stand and stare, with tears pouring down my cheeks; not of sadness, but pure joy and recognition. The Angel held out his hands to me. Both arms moved together in a gesture of giving and receiving. His hair moved, his robe moved, he was absolutely real.

Then the Angel turned to his side and drifted away into the sky. I thought my heart would stop and wanted to call out for him to take me with him, but remembered that we do have to be careful what we wish for and anyway, there was work to do!

A few seconds later, a large cerise-coloured heart appeared in the sky in front of my window where the Angel had been, as if someone had drawn it with a gigantic marker pen.

Was that for me? Or was I supposed to give my heart to others? As I watched, I panicked. I didn't want to fail this beautiful celestial messenger in my ignorance. I heard no voice, no instructions, no wonderful music, no trumpets. I suddenly felt terribly inadequate, as though I should have known what to do.

Then it came to me like a warm glow: I knew that the heart was the Angel's signature. I was working with Angels from the realms of pure love – Universal, Divine Love – and it was this message I was destined to share.

Although Chrissie did not describe the Angel as her Guardian Angel, when I asked her if I could use her story in this book, I explained why I thought that this amazing vision had revealed the beauty of her very own Beloved. The clue for me was in the words, 'I recognised him ... and he knew me too'. Her description of the immense feeling of love permeating every cell of her body was also, to me, a sign that she had experienced the presence of her Guardian, because the recognition is always accompanied by the certainty of being loved for yourself alone, without any conditions or judgements.

2

Help in Times of Change and Crisis

Ancient meetings

The Hebrew word for an Angel is *malakh,* a messenger, who often appears as an ordinary person. There are lots of biblical stories in which individuals are guided or protected by mysterious strangers, one well-known example concerns Joseph (*Genesis* 37: 15–17) who was hated by his jealous brothers because their father, Jacob, had given him the famous multicoloured coat. In the story, Joseph set off to find his brothers who were feeding their flocks. Called 'a dreamer' by his family, he wandered around aimlessly, not knowing how to find the others, who were proud of their practical abilities as shepherds. Then a 'certain man' found Joseph and asked: 'What seekest thou?' When Joseph explained that he needed to find his brothers, the 'man' directed him. Joseph found his brothers, who beat him up and sold him to slave traders travelling to Egypt. Eventually, Joseph's ability to interpret dreams made him useful to the Pharaoh. These events are crucial to the history of the Jewish people. If Joseph had not been sent on his way by this 'man', he might not have been sold into slavery, but then there would not have been the famous Exodus either – or the Ten Commandments, as received by Moses. So many generations later, the rabbis decided that the 'man' must have been Joseph's Guardian Angel, appearing in human form to make sure Joseph's destiny was kept on track.

I love the story of the prophet, Bala'am, and his poor donkey (*Numbers* 22: 12–35). In those old biblical tales, the Israelites were always at war with their neighbours and invariably seemed to win. They claimed this was because their god was more powerful than other gods. King Balak of Moab saw that the kings of nearby lands had lost their battles and tried to persuade Bala'am to curse Israel. Bala'am sent back word that he could only do what God commands and he had dreamed that under no circumstances should he support an enemy of Israel. But King Balak was not a quitter! He sent his High Priests to offer Bala'am great honours. Bala'am replied that he would not disobey God, even for a house full of silver and gold. Then God agreed that Bala'am could go to see King Balak, but only if he listened carefully to divine orders. Unfortunately, Bala'am set off without waiting to hear all of God's instructions. God was not at all happy, so He sent an Angel to block the prophet's path. This Angel was called a *satan* in Hebrew, which means an adversary. At first, the Angel only revealed himself to Bala'am's donkey which, faced with an Angel wielding a sword, ran into a nearby vineyard. Bala'am hit the poor animal, hoping to bully her back on to the path, but the Angel moved to cover the exit and there were walls on both sides. The donkey crushed herself against the wall and put all her weight on Bala'am's foot, so he hit her again! The Angel continued to block the pathway and the donkey fell down under Bala'am, whose fury was beyond control. Then God allowed the donkey to complain, using human language. She told Bala'am that she had always been loyal and didn't deserve to be beaten. Balaam had no idea what was going on – he was not very insightful, for a prophet! Eventually, God allowed Bala'am to see the Angel, at which point he understood that he had overstepped his role. He had not been truly mindful of the task in hand and had rushed ahead.

The really important moral in this story is that, when we fail to take heed of the messages we receive from our 'God' or from that wise 'other half' who abides within the deep recesses of our heart, we may face unexpected calamities. Our Guardian's task is to open up the path that is best for us and discourage us from taking wrong turnings. If we set off down an unsuitable track, we may well meet the *satan* aspect of our Guardian – the Angel as adversary. We may call it 'bad luck', but there is always a good metaphysical reason underpinning all 'luck', good or bad.

Visions and voices

Biblical prophets were usually very keen to achieve visionary states. They fasted and spent days and nights alone in the desert. They knew these techniques would lead them to heightened states of consciousness and they wanted to commune with God, or, at least, to meet an Angel. Many of the experiences we can read about in the Hebrew Scriptures, as well as in the apocryphal texts that were excluded from the Bible, came about because the Israelite prophets were hoping to find out what God wanted, so the tribe could follow the rules and keep in favour. The prophets were playing a similar role to the shaman, accessing higher realms in order to help the tribe survive. A shaman is someone who deliberately cultivates altered states of consciousness and brings back his visions or dreams to the rest of the community. But not all visions – including messages from Angels – are invited. Sometimes they arrive out of the blue and the mystical journey is initiated suddenly, without any prior warning. On some occasions the visionary resists the calling, realising that it may be tough. Moses, for example, was a very reluctant prophet who, even after hearing God's voice from a burning bush (*Exodus* 3: 1–6), tried to dodge out of his mission by saying he was slow of speech (scholars believe he may have had a stammer), but God told him to get his brother Aaron to speak for him (*Exodus* 4: 10–16).

In *Judges* (6: 11–40), Gideon was a hard-working farmer. His tribe was suffering because local Midianites were stealing their crops. When an Angel turned up, saying, 'The Lord is with you, valiant warrior', Gideon was sceptical. He kept asking for evidence that the message was really from an Angel sent by God. The Angel obliged on three separate occasions: first he touched Gideon's offering of bread and meat with his staff and it burst into flames. Then, when Gideon left a fleece on the floor overnight, the dew fell only on the fleece and not on the ground around it. Finally, apparently just to be perverse, Gideon asked for the opposite to happen: dew on the ground and not on the fleece. The Angel duly obliged – sometimes they have to be very patient with us!

When the Prophet Mahomet received a visit from Gabriel, the Archangel commanded him to 'recite'. Like Moses, the Prophet felt he was not up to the task but went on to write down the most beautiful, divinely inspired poetry that is found in the Koran. This spiritual book became a focus for nomadic tribes, who gathered under the Prophet's banner and became a powerful Islamic nation.

Joan of Arc was visited by the Archangel Michael, who told her she was destined to save France from English invaders. Joan seemed to welcome her Angels without question. Perhaps she was keen to get away from her menial duties as a country girl. Her mission was such a powerful driving force that she went against all the social conventions of her day and dressed as a soldier, leading the Dauphin's forces into battle.

Winston Churchill never mentioned meeting an Angel when he was young, but as a small boy he did announce to his school friends that he was going to save Britain. Later, as Prime Minister, he would often undertake walkabouts during the Blitz, telling his bodyguard, Walter Thompson, that he was protected by heavenly powers. A number of close shaves convinced Thompson that this was true.

It is very noticeable that people whose names go down in the history books often 'know' their destiny very early, having a powerful conviction that seems to be backed up by unswerving faith in their own 'genius'. They believe they are supported by something beyond rational explanation. We can see from some of the stories above that many angelic events seem to occur when tribal or national survival is in question. I am sure that the Angels do not have favourite countries that they support, but the overall survival of the human race is a natural concern of theirs, so their energy will be available to anyone who seeks to create peace and harmony. People who are driven to overthrow or escape from despotic rulers, whether they are pharoahs, kings or dictators, often seem to get help from celestial realms.

Stories from survivors and lonely travellers

In 1916, after Sir Ernest Shackleton made his historic, life-threatening journey across the Antarctic with two of his companions, all three men recalled the constant impression of the presence of a fourth, invisible 'man' among them. This famous story of 'spiritual sustenance' on a journey is not as rare as we might think. When we are thrown back on our own resources, because the usual comforts and structures of civilisation are not in place, we often ask for support from invisible worlds, and there are plenty of stories from travellers to confirm that this help is readily available.

Over the last few years, there have been many reports from people who have received help from strangers under difficult circumstances, especially when they have been stranded late at night, feeling frightened and alone. The American Angel writer, Joan Wester Anderson, has collected many such stories (consult her website for a list of her titles – see Recommended websites, p. 224). The popularity of Joan's books and others like them have helped to convince more people that Angels do help us in practical ways.

Joan tells the story of Alice who went to visit a friend in her new home town. Later that afternoon, she set off to return home but, because she didn't know the public transport system there, after getting off the first bus and waiting for an hour and a half she discovered that the last connecting bus on a Sunday had already left. This was in the days before mobile phones, but Alice managed to find a public phone, thinking she could call her father to pick her up – only to discover she had no change. The phone was in a deserted building. It was getting dark and beginning to snow outside. All she needed was a dime. So she started to pray. Quite suddenly, a young man turned up. He was not dressed for winter weather and there was no sign of snow on him. 'You look like you could use a dime,' he said, smiling, and dropped one into her hand. Alice thanked him and turned towards the phone, but then wondered how he had arrived so silently. When she turned back, there was no sign of anyone – but she was able to make the telephone call.

Tales from scenes of accidents and great danger

There are many stories from hospitals and the scenes of accidents that confirm the protective and healing roles of our Guardian Angels. In her book, *Angels of Mercy*, Rosemary Guiley, an American Angel researcher, recounts a story told to her by a Californian woman:

AIMEE'S STORY

Aimee was suffering from a rare throat virus that caused her to cough violently, so she would feel as though she was being strangled. During one of these fits in the middle of the night, she called for a nurse but no one came and she began to panic. Suddenly, the door flew open and a short, stocky nurse burst in. In a voice of authority, she instructed Aimee to close her mouth and breathe through her nose. Aimee gestured that no air could come through her nose, but the nurse clamped a firm hand over Aimee's mouth and shouted, 'Breathe!' Aimee had no choice but to breathe through her nose and the choking stopped. The nurse said, 'I can't understand why they haven't taught you that,' and promptly left. When Aimee asked about the nurse the next morning, hoping to thank her, no one on the ward recognised her description of the night visitor. None of the nursing staff seemed to understand the technique Aimee had learned for preventing choking, but the doctor did admit that he knew it. Although he didn't explain why no one had taught Aimee what to do in an emergency, he leaned over and said in a whisper: 'I think it was an Angel that visited you.'

In my experience, nurses are generally more prepared to talk about unusual visitations and mysterious helpers than doctors, who are probably more inclined to scepticism. Certainly, modern medical training does not favour interest in the subtle realms of human experience. But I did hear a story from one doctor who admitted he'd had what he felt was supernatural assistance on several occasions during his medical work. I was giving a talk to a progressive Jewish group, and I think it is fair to say that progressive and liberally minded Jews are generally not much interested in the Angels; they seem to consider such ideas as antiquated kabbalistic mysticism, which they think of as a relic from a bygone age. So I was surprised when this doctor gave an account of one particular experience that had occurred when he was attempting to give a life-saving injection to a teenage boy who was having an epileptic seizure. The boy was thrashing about and, because he was also overweight, placing the needle correctly was a serious challenge for the doctor. Just when he felt he was going to fail in his attempt to deliver the necessary medication, the doctor felt a firm, but invisible, hand on his wrist and 'someone' pushing his hand so that the needle went in to the correct place.

Stories of invisible hands helping in an emergency often crop up in angelic encounters. Another story told in *Angels of Mercy* describes how Robert, an industrial electrician, grabbed a high-voltage wire that he didn't know was live. As he felt the electricity surge through his body he thought, quite simply, My God, I don't want to die! Instantly, he was pulled off the wire by invisible hands that grabbed him around his waist. He was hurled violently across the floor and came round to see his co-workers gazing down at him, wondering why he wasn't dead. Two years after the accident, Robert suffered from psoriasis – itchy skin patches – around his waist, just where he had felt those angelic hands; the hands of his Guardian Angel, he believes.

WILL'S STORY

In 1982, my husband Will borrowed a neighbour's car while our own Citroën was at the garage, having a new gearbox fitted. The borrowed car was a large, old Ford, which had a very bouncy suspension system, compared with the responsive one in the Citroën. The difference in the suspension may account for Will's inability to handle the car. Whatever the reason, on the way home, when taking a familiar bend in a country road, Will found himself losing control of the car, which started rocking from side to side, before rolling over and somersaulting across the road into the lane reserved for oncoming traffic. It was early evening in the autumn and it was getting dark. Fortunately, there was not a great deal of traffic.

Will suddenly found himself out of his body, a few hundred feet up in the air. From that vantage point, he could see the Ford spinning across the road, but also saw the lights of a car coming towards it from the opposite direction. He heard a voice saying, 'Don't worry, no one is going to get hurt.' Then, quite suddenly, he returned to his body, not in the driver's seat, but curled up in the back of the car. The car had come to a halt, upside down and with most of the roof squashed flat. The windows were all shattered and Will crawled out through the back window, stood up and shook himself down. His only injuries were a few scratches from the glass on the road as he was leaving the car.

People from nearby cottages had gathered round the wreck. They had called an ambulance and were wondering about the fate of the driver. Will announced it was him, and was met with disbelief. This took place before wearing seat belts was made a legal requirement, so Will had not been strapped in to the front seat, otherwise he would surely have died. As for the car that had been coming the other way, it turned out to be carrying five elderly people. The large, heavy Ford had ploughed straight into the front of the little Vauxhall, but none of the occupants sustained any injuries, apart from one lady who bruised her shin slightly. The voice was right – no one was hurt.

I thought it was extraordinary that Will, who is six foot four, had managed to move from the front seat – which had a bulky headrest that filled up much of the space between the seat and the roof – into the back seat, while the car was somersaulting across the road. And while Will, by his own account, was not even in his own body! When we talked about the 'voice', Will said he thought perhaps it sounded like his own voice, but that the statement, 'No one is going to get hurt' had been delivered with such authority and certainty that he'd felt, somehow, he was in good hands.

Even in concentration camps people have felt protected by their Guardian Angel. Recently, I read the account of a woman who wanted to smuggle her Bible and her personal underwear under the skimpy garments supplied by the guards. She had to get past the rigorous process set up by the Nazi security. But her faith was a powerful ally and she called inwardly on God's angelic forces to protect her from scrutiny. Everyone in front of her and beside her, including her sister, was thoroughly checked from head to toe, but she walked through unnoticed. Even under the most terrifying circumstances humans can rely on angelic support, even if all the angels can do is help us meet our death in a state of spiritual grace and ecstasy.

Near-death experiences

Raymond Moody's book, *Life after Life*, first published in 1975, brought near-death experiences (NDEs) to public attention for the first time, and these often included a meeting with 'beings of light' or Angels. Since then, extensive research has collated many hundred of stories from people who were brought back to life after a life-threatening event, such as a cardiac arrest. Some people feel they have met their Guardian Angel, who tells them they must return to life, even if it might feel easier to die.

My research into spiritual experiences (2000–2010) with the Alister Hardy Research Centre (see Recommended websites p. 224) included studying many near-death experiences (NDEs). However, in 1973, long before I had even heard about NDEs, I was making costumes for a local theatre and, while we were sitting around the large table doing some sewing, the wardrobe mistress, a middle-aged widow called Joan, described her own near-death experience:

> ## JOAN'S STORY
>
> Joan's husband had died in the Second World War, leaving her with two small children. Shortly after the war, she became ill with flu and inadvertently overdosed on paracetamol. The nurses believed Joan was in a coma, but when she came round she reported a beautiful experience in which she found herself going through a tunnel towards a source of light, where two figures in white were waiting. One of them spoke to her gently and said she had a choice: they could take her with them and she would be reunited with her husband, or she could return to her children. If she returned, they said, she would not meet her husband for a very long time. Joan knew her children needed her, so she returned to her physical body and regained her health.

At the time I heard this story, Joan's children were grown up. Although the event had happened nearly thirty years earlier, when Joan described it I could feel that the experience was as alive in her heart as though it had been yesterday. Many years after hearing this story I bumped into Jackie by chance in a gallery, and she told me her mother had recently died, at the age of eighty-six. I reminded Jackie what her mum had told me about her NDE and we both agreed that the celestial advisors had been right – it had been a very long time (nearly sixty years) before Joan had passed over to be reunited with her husband.

Birth announcements

The near-death stories reassure us that Angels watch over us as we die, but they also support us when we come into the world. I have come to believe that the Angels who appeared to announce the forth-coming birth of children who were destined to be important prophets or teachers must have been their Guardian Angels, and that they wanted to prepare the future mother for her special role as parent to a remarkable person. The stories of angelic visitations before the births of Isaac (*Genesis* 18: 10–14), Samson (*Judges* 13: 3), John the Baptist (*Luke* 1: 13) and Jesus (*Luke* 1: 30–31) are all good examples of a surprise visitation, often to a woman who does not expect to become pregnant, either because she is too old or not married.

I am also sure that any Soul who wants to incarnate will send a message to its new parents and some people experience visits from winged messengers in the shape of birds or butterflies. I have had such visits myself. In the 1960s, when I had my first two daughters, I wasn't particularly interested in looking or listening for other-worldly messages. Even in the mid-1970s, when I was hoping to become pregnant, I would not have especially looked out for a 'sign'. But then, in 1976, something very special occurred when I was sewing in my dressmaking workroom. Will had just gone out to fetch some lunch and everything was quiet. It was a beautiful autumn day, so the window was open. Something prompted me to look up from my sewing and there, sitting on the window ledge, was a little yellow bird; I guess it was a canary. It looked at me with its bright eyes, came inside, did a quick circuit above my head and vanished through the window. Immediately, I knew that it meant I was pregnant and, sure enough, our Gemini daughter was born in June the following year. I have often thought that a yellow bird was a very good sign for a Gemini baby – so bright and chirpy.

A few years later, when I was *not* planning any more children, I had another winged visitor. In December of 1980, I was practising advanced meditation techniques for an hour and a half, twice a day. One morning I was sitting on the bed with my eyes closed, prac-tising my mantra. It was pretty cold so the windows were definitely closed. After a few moments of quiet meditation I became aware of a fluttering around my face and opened my eyes to see a red admi-ral butterfly dancing in the air in front of me; I closed my eyes again and when I came out of my meditation there was no sign of it. I went down to the kitchen and told Will – perhaps, I said, it was another baby message (although I wasn't sure at that time whether it was a message I wanted to hear). But to our delight, our daughter was born the following October and a butterfly seemed to be a very suitable messenger for the beautiful little Libran girl who fluttered into our lives.

All these old biblical stories and modern-day reports confirm the presence of helping hands and spiritual guidance that is available to each of us as a constant resource. We do not need to be at death's door or want to save our country in order to develop a relationship with our Guardian Angel. Why should we wait until we are in trouble, before calling for help? If we talk to our Guardian on a regular basis we won't have so many problems (or headaches, as the Assyrians suggested). Our Guardian can help us to steer our ship of life, can be our navigator or first mate, so that we travel smoothly through life and practicalities become less of a burden. At a spiritual level, our Guardian is calling us to develop our potential, to become much more than we can imagine – to go beyond our limitations and flourish as truly divine beings, enjoying the full beauty of life on Earth.

3

A Vision For Your Future

... as Angels in some brighter dreams
call to the soul when man doth sleep ...

HENRY VAUGHAN

Changes for humanity – that includes you

I am writing this chapter in December 2009, almost exactly three years before the magical date of 21 December 2012 that has been logged in the ancient Mayan calendar as the end of the current age, and which many people believe will herald the arrival of a new era for humanity and planet Earth as a whole. Despite the dramatic, Armageddon-style movie, *2012*, the Mayan predictions for this historical turning point do not necessarily include major geological disasters that wipe the human race from the face of the Earth (see Recommended websites, p. 224, for more information). However, there are 'signs and wonders' which indicate we are moving through a transition into a potentially challenging new future. These signs are all around us: our planet is suffering and our present economic and social structures are shaky, but at the same time millions of people, even in poor countries, have access to internet technology enabling ordinary householders to communicate with each other at very high speed from every corner of the world. We can organise community projects that may include just our local catchment areas or global initiatives that reach out across the oceans to other continents. Social networking through the worldwide web allows us to take back power that has previously been only in the hands of giant corporations and governments. This is not simply a radical 'political' process, but a reclaiming of our spiritual birthright to be self-directed and to take personal responsibility for our lives. We can make enormous strides forward with the practical organisation of resources and there is no doubt, if we have the will and the commitment, that we can change our world for the better.

Effective and lasting practical changes depend, however, on more subtle realignments: our heartfelt desires, clear and wise thought processes and compassionate feelings. We all need to turn our attention away from the outer trappings of material success and status towards the inner achievements that provide the real building blocks for humanity's future. And this is where our Guardian Angels can step in, as cheerleaders and spiritual life coaches. In Jewish mysticism there is a phrase, *tikkun olam*, usually translated as 'the repairing (or completing) of the world'. This mystical idea suggests that God needs humans to contribute to the completion of His plan: Creation was not perfect to begin with, so our loving participation in the Divine Plan is absolutely necessary for healing the world. This concept, of co-creation, in which human beings are God's co-workers, can be found in the teachings of Isaac Luria, a mystic who lived over 500 years ago. What we need to know, in order to support this process of change and spiritual development, is how it will affect us and what we should be doing, as individuals and as communities. As Gandalf said to Frodo in Tolkein's *Fellowship of the Ring*: 'We need to decide what we will do with our time.' Remember, Frodo, although he felt lonely and often exhausted by the great task he had been given, was supported all the way by his constant companion, the practical Sam Gamgee. We all need to feel the support, not only from our fellow humans, but also from the higher power that sustains life; and, even if we often feel we are alone, our Guardian Angel is always at our side.

Your Guardian Angel and spiritual understanding

Many people who begin a spiritual quest are starting from a place of loss, or a sense of loneliness – perhaps a feeling that something is missing. I believe this is because most human beings have lost touch with the wise, all-knowing, divine part of themselves. For the most part, we function as half a person; the other half of us is like a rejected lover, banging on the door of our heart and rarely being heard. When we do listen to our Beloved – perhaps because we finally turned off the constant everyday chatter of our life, or maybe a crisis made us feel vulnerable and we cried out for help – we are surprised by the love that is freely available, like a constant fountain of water. For many, this is so surprising and amazing that the experience is dismissed, or brushed over, as not being 'real'. After all, to rely on this divine, boundless love would be 'too easy'; how much more 'sensible' to carry on doing things the hard way.

While I am writing this I am staying in my daughter's house and, as she is away for the weekend, I was on duck duty this morning. As soon as I woke up, I put on my dressing gown and boots and went out into a bright, frosty morning to open the duck house. The ducks waddled down to the river, quacking loudly and preened themselves in the water, dipping and fluttering their feathers. I watched them with great delight, thinking how simple it seems, to be almost any other creature than a human. How difficult we have made life for ourselves, being so ambitious to improve our skills and take more control over our environment.

Naturally, humans, like all other creatures, want to survive, and we want to feel safe and secure. But we have made a very big mistake, thinking that we have to use our physical bodies and man-made tools in order to redesign the world to fit our requirements. What we really need to rearrange is the way we think, then our world will mirror our thoughts and our lives will be beautiful – and simple. If we only think with our human half we will get a half-baked result; when we collaborate with our divine Beloved, our Guardian Angel, then the results we desire will arrive effortlessly. Perhaps a better word than 'collaborate' would be 'cohabit', which means 'to live together', as in a marriage in which we become 'as one flesh'. Our marriage vows would not include 'for better and for worse' because in this relationship things can only get better; nor would we say 'for richer, for poorer' because 'poverty' cannot be found in the divine dictionary. What our vows would include are the following words:

❖ I trust you completely.

❖ I surrender my small self to you.

❖ I acknowledge my failings with grace.

❖ I accept your unconditional love.

❖ I open my heart to joy, delight and abundance.

❖ I dedicate my life to an intimate relationship with you.

❖ Our life together will shine like a beacon, beckoning others to accept the Divine Love that is their birthright.

And each promise will be a gift, not a burden.

Seeing the world in a new light

In many cultures, spiritual development is seen as a journey in which the Soul is on a path, sometimes across a wasteland or up a mountain, where the terrain is difficult. We stumble and trip, sometimes lose our direction and even turn back to our old ways, finding those comfortable habits easier to live with.

One traditional story tells how a spiritual seeker looked back over his life and noticed that, next to his own footprints in the sand was a second set of prints, as though he had always been under the invisible protection of his Guardian Angel who walked beside him. But when he looked closely, he noticed that sometimes the extra footprints disappeared and he wondered whether this spiritual help was reliable. He asked out loud, 'Why, when I was in times of sadness and despair, did you abandon me?' The answer that came back to him was: 'The times when you only see one set of footprints in the sand are the times when I was carrying you.'

It is your own choice whether to believe that divine companionship is available to you and, if you abandon doubt and place your trust in this possibility, your life will change beyond all recognition. With your heartfelt co-operation, your Guardian will be able to help you race along your spiritual path, your feet hardly touching the ground, and the obstacles you thought were in your way will disappear. You will leave behind a limited, narrow way of experiencing life and, like Dorothy in *The Wizard of Oz* movie, you will step out of a black and white world into a paradise, where everything is in Technicolor. You just have to allow your old concepts to fall away – hopefully it won't take a tornado for you to see through the door into a magical new world!

Will you step out of the old you and into the new?

The God of the Hebrew Bible is very unfashionable nowadays. He has always had a reputation for being a vengeful and jealous dictator who would wreak havoc with human lives if He lost patience. But some of the things God said to the biblical prophets, who lived as long as 5000 years ago, still contain powerful messages for us today. The most important thing God told Moses – repeated to later

prophets, like Isaiah – is that 'God is One'. This message is fundamental to our understanding of the creative process – that the
creative intelligence that sustains the universe is 'One'. Underneath
the apparent diversity and multiplicity of Creation, from the galaxies, to the rocks and trees, flowers, animals, birds and our own
human selves, is a unified field of energy, constantly creating and
renewing the world we see around us. This Oneness not only fuels
the universe, but initiates the patterns found in cellular structures
down to the smallest life form.

When we truly realise that the Oneness of God, or whatever
word you like to use for divine power, is the source of our existence,
then we can participate in the creative process as co-creators. Our
Guardian Angels will open the portals to this realisation when we
are ready to step into this new way of being.

God gave Moses a prayer for the Israelites, to use as a daily
reminder of this Oneness: 'Hear, Oh Israel! The Lord thy God is One'
(*Deuteronomy* 6: 4–11). In Hebrew, the first word in this prayer is
shema and Jewish people throughout the centuries have said the
Shema when they get up in the morning and when they go to bed.
It is the pious desire of every devout Jew to be able to say the *Shema*
as their last words on their deathbed. 'Israel' (meaning 'he who struggles with God') was the name given to the tribe after Jacob had his
night-time struggle with an Angel. So the prayer is addressed to
anyone who struggles, or wrestles, with God, and serves as a
reminder to listen and realise that God is One. We all feel as though
we are separate individuals, experiencing the world through our five
senses; and our world is full of millions of other separate humans as
well as animals, plants, rocks and stars – but the underlying creative
energy that sustains us is a unity. Once this is realised, and we accept
the grace and love of God, there will be no need to struggle any
more. In addition, God promised abundance and comfort, saying
what we need will come effortlessly: 'You will live in houses that you
have not built, with vineyards that you have not planted' (*Exodus* 30:
20–23). All we have to do is constantly reconnect with the Oneness
and life will become comfortable, very simple and stress free.

But the Oneness is enormous and scary. Moses was told that he could not see God face to face (*Exodus* 4: 10–16) because the endless power and vast energy of the Universal Creator is too much for an individual person to experience first hand. The idea that we should abandon the safety of our everyday coping self will probably fill us with trepidation. We human beings like our comfort zones. This is why we need the loving support of the Angels, who can create bridges between our everyday selves and the Divine Source of our being. Our Guardian Angel holds our hand in this process, gently taking us towards Oneness so that we feel safe and are able to ground the experience in our day-to-day lives. 'If thine eye be single, then shall thy whole body be full of light', said Jesus (*Matthew* 6: 22), telling us that we need to focus with one eye – our third eye – and not be distracted by the dualism of a pair of eyes that constantly criticises and compares. When we experience the unified field, instead of the diversity of Creation, then we are filled with the light of God, which rushes through us like a wind, revealing the truth and beauty of Creation.

Are you ready to make that step? Every human being has the capacity to become a truly remarkable, 200 per cent person – 100 per cent divine, 100 per cent human. If only 10 per cent of people on our planet renewed their vows of intimacy with their beloved Guardian Angels and turned towards the light of God, then humanity as a whole would be transformed. If not now, when?

Then let us begin ...

4

Your Divine Life Coach

Last night I woke
And saw an Angel
Seated on my bed.

THEOLYN CORTENS

No voice? No shining figure?

Many quite ordinary people report miraculous events and unexpected visions for which the activity of a guardian spirit or Angel seems to be the best explanation. The owner of the voice Will heard during his car accident (see page 21) clearly knew a great deal more about what was going to happen than Will did. But do Guardian Angels speak so clearly to everyone? People who report seeing shining figures, experiencing a sense of wonder and reassurance, do not always receive a message in words. The Angel Chrissie saw in the sky (see page 11) had responded to her plea; she was longing to see something with her own eyes. But what if there is no serious crisis or dramatic event in your life? What if you don't hear a voice, apparently coming from nowhere? What if you don't see a majestic being of light? How can you trust the idea that you have a personal guide, if nothing obvious has happened to make you notice divine guidance or intervention?

The answer is that guidance does not have to be dramatic or obvious. When I run workshops or give talks, I always find people can identify small clues, strange happenings or prompts that have occurred over the years, as though somewhere, deep inside, they have a guiding compass. If you consider your own life story, you will probably recall moments that have had a particular flavour to them, something odd that makes them stick in your memory. Even if you have not been aware of a 'being' of any kind, you may have felt 'led' in one direction, rather than another. These inner promptings often happen at key turning points in one's life and they can be so subtle that they may be easily dismissed as a fancy or a trick of the mind. Sometimes, they have seemingly been initiated not by an inner whisper, but by something from outside. Perhaps a friend, parent, teacher or colleague has said something, or an unexpected event has provoked you to make a particular choice. A missed train, a chance meeting, a notice in a shop window – these can all be signs that your Guardian Angel is at work, steering you in a certain direction without your conscious awareness.

I find the best way to help students to identify these moments is to have them draw a timeline of their lives, starting at the point when their parents first met. Most people have heard how their parents came together and this is obviously a very significant event, as it tells us a great deal about the people involved. What might appear to have been a chance meeting invariably has another layer underlying it, a driving force that makes the union inescapable, just so that you can be born. Even if your parents subsequently split up, the key moment that led to your existence is crucial and the occasion is tinged with the quality and flavour that fit your requirements.

For instance, my parents met at a concert in Westminster Abbey and, although I wasn't brought up in any religious tradition, I have spent a lot of my life studying comparative religion and writing books about Angels. Westminster Abbey is also the resting place of the great English poets; my parents had a love of poetry in common and poetry is the other important thread in my life. I was named Theolyn, not for religious reasons, but after my grandmother whose name was Theoline. (Sadly, Theoline died when my mother was five years old, so I never met her.) My name means 'river (or stream) of God' and this is entirely suitable for my Soul's purpose. It is very close in meaning to the Hebrew word *shefa*, which means the flow of Divine Energy. I didn't realise this connection when I was first inspired to use the word *shefa* for the healing that I offer, but when I did notice this, I thought how amazing it is that everything we do is an outer reflection of our inner essence.

The name you have been given is no 'coincidence' and astrologers say they can find significators for a person's name in their birth chart. So, while you are doing your timeline, you could also check out what your name means and how it was chosen. Consider whether you feel it is really suitable for you or whether you might want to change your name, once you have begun to experience a new way of being in the world. Your Guardian Angel could help you choose a new name, if that seems the best way forward.

The following exercise can have a profound effect on your understanding of your life, and the events and people who have played a part in your story so far. Once you have put down the basic outline, you can add to it whenever you want. Reviewing your life in this way is like collecting the pieces of a jigsaw – first you find the edges, then you collect the blue pieces for the sky, then the green ones for the trees and so on. Gradually, an outline is put in place, the details begin to emerge and you start to see the connections.

Starting out on the research for your personal timeline can prompt you to ask questions of your family. Sometimes you will receive helpful answers, sometimes there may be evasions. 'Skeletons in the cupboard' are particular areas of interest, as the very things that families want to hide may well be the most important signposts in your life. Be persistent – if pieces in your puzzle seem to be missing, then keep looking.

Exercise: Your Timeline

Treat this as an ongoing exploration that can be added to over time, as necessary.

1. You will need a long, narrow piece of plain paper. You could tape together several sheets of ordinary A4 paper along their short sides. I suggest taking one sheet for each complete decade or part of a decade of your life. For example, if you are thirty-four years old, you will need four sheets. This is only a rough guide; if you start work and don't have enough space, just add more paper. An alternative is to use a roll of plain wallpaper, the kind used to line walls. In this case, mark off a fixed length for each decade – this will allow you to create an even layout, although some decades may well become more crammed than others.

The timeline of your life

    You will also need a soft pencil, an eraser and some coloured pencils or felt pens. The pencil can be used to sketch your timeline in outline, making alterations with the eraser as necessary, before using your colours for highlighting obvious connections.

2. Allow yourself a quiet evening on your own. Turn off the phones and put out any cats or dogs, as they might be keen to join in!

Although you may be tempted to play some relaxing music, I recommend doing this kind of exercise in silence, because you are trying to recall important events, some of which may be stuck deep in your memory. Quiet musing with no distractions allows thoughts to rise up from your unconscious. During your reappraisal of your life up until now, it is quite possible that a new perspective or understanding may arrive 'out of the blue' – a thought or notion that has not crossed your mind before. You will begin to see how the pattern of your life story has unfolded.

3. Lay out your paper on the dining-room table, or on the floor if you prefer, and draw a line along its length, a little way up from the bottom. The space below the line will be for entering dates; the space above is where you will add comments, notes and any other useful details. These comments and dates can be written at right angles to the line to give you more space. At first, you will just mark in the dates and the basic information; then you can go back over it, adding details. Start at the left-hand end of the line and mark your first date, using the earliest possible event you can identify. Ideally, this would be when your parents first met or when you were conceived. If you haven't already heard how and when your parents met, I suggest you ask them; if they are no longer alive, there may be a relation or family friend who knows the story. Otherwise, put in your earliest known date.

4. When you have put in your first date, spend a few moments with your eyes closed, bringing to mind any significant events you remember, or have been told about, that occurred during your first ten years. These events do not have to have any special feelings associated with them; they can be quite mundane – for example, perhaps your parents moved house when you were two years old. Whatever occurred, just note the dates on the line. Then do the same for the next decade and so on. Continue along the paper, marking all the events that come to mind, such as:

- ❖ Mum and Dad divorced when I was five.

- ❖ I went to the seaside for a holiday with my aunt while Mum was in hospital giving birth to my sister.

- ❖ I broke my leg.

- ❖ My school chose me to lead the cricket team.

- ❖ We went to Scotland and I saw Loch Ness.

- ❖ I met my future wife, Janet. She was making teas at the village cricket match.

- ❖ Janet and I married in Glasgow, her home town.

- ❖ My first child was born.

Carry on as far as you can go, up to the present day, leaving gaps between events so that they are spaced out across the length you have allowed for each decade.

Now go back over your timeline, filling in any more information you think of. When you have completed as much as you can for the first session, roll up your timeline like a scroll and tie it with a ribbon. It is a very important document!

After completing the exercise above, you are likely to dream some helpful dreams, which may bring up further memories, and in the days that follow you will find you want to add to your timeline. Once your dates are firmed up and you don't need to make changes, use colours to highlight any repeating themes, places or activities. Colours can also be used to mark really important points, whether highs or lows. Gold stars might be useful, for shining moments. You may find yourself becoming rather obsessive! This can be helpful, as your mind will respond to your determination to uncover any important pieces in the pattern. Once you feel you have a good picture in place, put your scroll away in a safe place, somewhere special. Treat it with reverence. You could place it on a mantelpiece next to a photograph of yourself as a baby, then light a small candle beside it (don't leave candles unattended).

My students' reports

The students in the eClass agreed that drawing their timeline was a challenging task. Some found it difficult to remember significant occasions; some didn't want to look at the more unhappy events. I explained that the idea of the timeline is to get an overall picture and develop a sense of the *story* of your life, with its ups and downs, and to see any patterns that you may have been repeating.

Veronique, a French student, said she did experience some resistance to starting her timeline, wondering whether she really wanted to revisit painful experiences. But then she found she was able to stay calm and centred while she looked at the first twenty years of her life – the good and not-so-good memories. She told the group she was very inspired by the project and thought she would keep her timeline constantly updated, so that it could be a record of her life to pass down to her children.

Torunn, a Norwegian student, also encountered some resistance, but asked her Guardian Angel to be with her for emotional support. She was able to feel calm and was interested to see what she might uncover that she had forgotten.

Helen, from England, said that part of her was not very enthusiastic about the idea at first, but when she looked back at the first twenty-five years of her life, she was amazed to see how often her grandmother's name cropped up. This helped her to realise what a wonderful background support her grandmother had been for her.

When I added my comment to the discussion board I put up a quotation from William Blake:

Joy and woe are woven fine
Clothing for the soul divine

Another Norwegian student, Bjørg, said she was surprised how many pages she could fill. The memories kept coming really quickly until she reached the last decade and after that, the process became slower as she started to review the spiritual changes of recent years. She saw that she had changed enormously since 2000 and was able to acknowledge her own progress towards spiritual maturity.

All the students realised that the timeline was an amazingly valuable document that they could keep going back to, reminding them that there is no such thing as a 'mistake', just happenings on our life path that are always part of our story. When we take this viewpoint, we are able to stop blaming ourselves and others. We can put our complaints to one side, allow the guilt to lift from our shoulders and begin to see our unhelpful patterns. Most importantly, we get the chance to spot those wonderful moments when we have been supported by our Guardian Angel.

TANYA'S STORY

In Britain during the Second World War there were many brief relationships that led to unplanned pregnancies. Sometimes, married women, whose husbands were away fighting, would have a 'fling' with a foreign soldier or a refugee and many babies were born who never met their fathers.

In 1939, Tanya's mum, Anne, a Lancashire housewife, already had three daughters aged between five and eight years old when her Scottish husband, Gordon Duncan, joined the army. Anne went to live in Kent with her unmarried sister, Mary, who was working as a Land Girl. The children went to the local school, Anne took a part-time job in a grocery shop and Mary offered occasional babysitting so that her sister could have some social life. Anne would sometimes go out in the evenings, visiting a nearby pub, where she met and fell in love with Jacob, a Russian Jewish refugee who had escaped from Berlin.

Jacob was younger than Anne. He had a deformed foot

which had made him unfit for service. He was unemployed and slept wherever he could find a bed, so Anne never had an address for him. As the romance developed, Jacob would sometimes sleep with Anne in Mary's home.

When Anne became pregnant, Jacob simply disappeared from the scene. Anne refused Mary's offer to pay for an abortion, which was illegal at the time and would have been dangerous. Mary told Anne to be honest with Gordon, but Anne felt it would be devastating for him to receive her news by post. However, Gordon was reported missing in action two months before Tanya was born and Anne was relieved that she never had to tell him about her adultery.

After the war finished, Anne took her four girls back to Lancashire. Tanya always knew she was the odd one out in the family; she constantly had to explain to other children why she was dark when all her siblings had red hair. She often embroidered the story, making her mysterious father a Russian prince who had to return home to rule his lands. The only real facts she knew were Jacob's surname (Kosikowsky) and that he came from Berlin. Anne had a single photograph of him, which gave Tanya some sense of connection. Tanya never felt close to her half-sisters and, as soon as she left school, she started to use Kosikowsky as her surname and moved to London to find work.

After Tanya changed her name, a number of important events unfolded. She took a job as a home help with a Jewish family and they put her in touch with an elderly refugee called Marie, who was researching missing Jews. Tanya didn't expect ever to find Jacob and wasn't actively hunting for him, but through Marie she discovered a whole family tree that she might never have known about if she had kept Duncan as her name. She learned Russian, which came easily to her, and began to earn better money as a translator.

It was twenty years before Tanya plucked up the courage actually to visit Berlin, where she found some younger members of the family and discovered that Jacob had never returned to Germany. She learned that he had been an artist and was fluent in several languages. One of his relatives gave her a self-portrait painted by Jacob that Tanya now treasures.

By drawing her timeline, Tanya could see the thread of her life with a fresh eye and recognise the connections that had brought her to her present situation. She felt she had been guided to change her name since this had enabled her to meet new relations who enriched her life, even though she never met Jacob.

The Fates and the Web of Wyrd

Ancient myths are full of mysterious characters who dictate that some people's lives must unfold as tragedies, while others are allowed to sail through life, accumulating wealth or recognition. Almost invariably, these powerful, inscrutable and relentless beings are female. In the Greek myths, the three Fates – Clotho, Lachesis and Atropos – spin, measure and finally cut the thread of life. Our Guardian Angels understand these invisible threads and, if we listen, will guide us towards positive outcomes.

The Norse myths feature the Norns – Urd, Verdandi and Skuld – who are female personifications of past, present and future, and they weave the 'Web of Wyrd'. *Wyrd* is an Old English and Norse word, which could be translated as 'fate' or 'destiny', but not in the sense of a predetermined future: each person has their *wyrd*, their true essence that allows them to create their own future. The Web of Wyrd is the tapestry of life, in which our individual stories, or *wyrds,* are woven into a greater picture. The strands of this invisible web are constantly criss-crossing and drawing together those people and events that need to be matched, so that all our individual *wyrds* can be fulfilled and the greater story manifested before the end of time. The Norns do not weave according to their own wishes, but serve as blind servants of Orlog, the eternal law of the universe. Orlog is depicted as an older, superior power with neither beginning nor end. Shakespeare's three witches, who tell Macbeth his future, are probably based on the Norns. Sometimes, when something odd happens and we suspect that a mysterious force might be at work, we call it 'weird' (which derives from *wyrd*) and Shakespeare's witches describe themselves as the 'weird sisters'.

These stories have developed because we humans feel powerless to determine the direction or length of our own lives; it's easier to believe that greater forces are at work, over which we have no control. Our main problem is that, instead of understanding our connection to the Oneness of Creation, we see ourselves as separate individuals, grappling with the unpredictable tides of life like so many lonely sailors in small, fragile boats with no compass and no navigator. We imagine the 'Fates' as fickle, if not cruel, picking us up or abandoning us with no apparent rhyme or reason.

The knowledge that we have a guiding light, in the shape of our Guardian Angel, frees us from the feeling that we are merely the puppets of supernatural powers. Also, when we gain a broader perspective, we can see our individual journey as part of the whole story of humanity and this understanding helps us to grow wiser. I believe we can also befriend our own personal navigator – our Guardian Angel or *daimon* – and that this relationship will allow us to steer a perfect course, based on a deeply rooted sense of purpose and intent. Every individual who is committed to their personal spiritual development is contributing to the evolution of human consciousness as a whole. Our Guardian Angels understand the invisible threads that connect us together and, if we listen, will guide us towards positive outcomes, not just for ourselves but for all human beings on our wonderful planet. This is why our Guardian Angels need us to work with them.

Special people, special events

Drawing a timeline helps bring important people and events to your attention. Often, it helps you to recall the way a certain person arrived in your life, provoking a significant new direction for you.

When I was ten years old, an actor who had retired to our village made an exciting donation to the primary school – a wicker basket full of theatrical costumes. I still remember the thrill when the basket was unpacked. This event encouraged me to write a play and have my school friends perform it. After that, I was always sewing costumes or dressing dolls in historical clothes. Later, I went to art school to study fashion design and went on to work in the wardrobe department of the Oxford Playhouse, before setting up my own business, creating wedding dresses and ball gowns.

Some events are notable because they bring our attention to the way 'fate' intervenes positively, saving us from getting involved in potentially disastrous situations.

CAROLYN'S STORY

In 1952, when Carolyn was eight years old, her family was living near Farnborough, home of the famous annual air show. Carolyn's mum and dad were keen to go to the show that year and their next-door neighbour, Derek, invited them to join him with Mark, his young son. They would have room in the car for Carolyn, her mum and dad and her younger brother. The show was to take place over the whole weekend and they agreed that Saturday would suit everyone best.

On Saturday morning, Derek came round to say that he had a problem with his car and would have to take it to the garage.

He was quite confident they would be able to go on Sunday, so no one would be disappointed.

That afternoon, Mark, who had been listening to a radio report of the air show, came running into Carolyn's house with news of a serious disaster. A plane had crashed into the crowd, killing the crew and twenty-nine spectators, as well as injuring many more.

When Carolyn recounted this story in a workshop, she told us how she remembered wondering whether the problem with the car had happened so that her family would not be killed at the air show.

Your timeline is a powerful tool in your quest for a deeper relationship with your Guardian Angel. Keep going back to it while you are working through the other exercises in this book. Gradually you will begin to form an overall picture of your story and why it has unfolded in a particular way. You will start to see the magic that underpins your life, even in the down moments. Getting this overview will make you realise that you have been the Captain of the ship all the time, even if you didn't really understand what you were doing. As you become more intimate with your Guardian Angel you will feel more and more confident about making effective decisions and creating a life that you love.

5

Meditation Is the Magic Ingredient

What though my hours of bliss have been,
Like angel-visits, few and far between?

THOMAS CAMPBELL

Becoming a 200 per cent person

Your Guardian Angel needs you to become a fully realised human being. Esoteric traditions say that once this has happened you won't need a Guardian Angel any more. This is because your Angel will then be so close to you that you will no longer feel its presence as a separate person; you will feel complete. When you first start experiencing this feeling, it can be quite surprising and a bit strange, although the feeling will come and go, sometimes staying with you for a day or so, then going for maybe as much as a few weeks. During that time you may feel like someone whose lover has gone overseas and you can't even get them on your mobile! But then the connection comes back, usually when you don't try too hard, and you realise that the only reason you were disconnected is because you were preoccupied with daily life in your old way of being.

The most important thing you can do in order to keep the line open to your Guardian Angel is to meditate. Meditation is not just important for you as an individual; by meditating you will be helping to create a better future for humanity.

When I learned Transcendental Meditation (TM) in the 1970s, I was told that the Maharishi, who brought it to the West, wanted to get 10 per cent of the human population to meditate and that this would create a quantum leap in the state of consciousness for all humanity. He explained that, in the past, the development of human consciousness was down to a few very powerful yogis, meditating constantly in their caves, hidden away in the mountain ranges of the East. He told us that, if it were not for these dedicated meditators, human beings would not still be here. Now, he said, it was up to ordinary householders all over the world to share the responsibility.

The minds of people who do not meditate are full of clutter, which creates stress for themselves and everyone around them. In the same way that we clear out unwanted information from our computers or mess from our rooms, our stress needs to be cleared on a regular basis. If we were sharing a house with other people, we would agree that everyone should share the washing up and the cleaning. Similarly, when we neglect our meditation practice, it is like leaving other people to do all the hard work, clearing up after us. Keeping our individual minds free of clutter allows us to focus properly on creating a wonderful life. If you are shining like a star because your mind is clear as a bell, you will be unstressed and happy, spreading joy wherever you go, and this will ripple out into the whole human race.

At a subtle level, when we meditate we are helping to clear the accumulation of old karmic rubbish that is blocking the progress of collective human consciousness. As we go deep into our meditation, we are able to heal our own ancestral and family wounds; as we go deeper still, we support the healing of the whole human race, which will enable us to create a new future in which humans live up to their full potential.

It was my TM teacher who introduced me to the Maharishi's notion that we can all live life as '200 per cent' people – 100 per cent human, physical beings with comfortable and abundant material welfare, plus 100 per cent spiritual beings with extraordinary abilities, such as healing powers, levitation, longevity, bi-location (being in two places at once) and other yogic skills. In ancient times, before the great Flood, the Bible tells us, there were remarkable people (the Nephalim) living on our planet who were the children of 'the sons of God' and 'the daughters of Earth'. Some say they were half Angel, half human. These Nephalim lived for hundreds of years and were described as gigantic in stature. With the Flood, much of their knowledge was lost, although it is very likely that some of the Nephalim managed to carry their knowledge and wisdom to small groups of survivors around the world. This wisdom is found in all the old mystical traditions. We can all aspire to becoming like these 200 per cent beings. Our goal must be to people the world with a new race of Nephalim, and the Guardian Angels of humanity are calling us all to take up this challenge. They *need* us to focus our attention on our highest possibility. Are you up for it?

Commitment

While our modern Western lifestyle tries to protect us from anything that might be considered too challenging, spiritual development *demands* challenges, so we need to move out of our comfort zone, shedding old habits that inhibit our progress, while taking on some positive new ones.

As you develop your relationship with your Guardian Angel, this transition begins to feel very simple and beautiful. Old thought patterns start to slip away until, one day, you start noticing that your mind is like a clear blue sky – the clarity and joy you experience will make you smile and chuckle. It's like being in love. Ask yourself the following questions:

What am I willing to give up?

❖ Using unsuitable food and drink as comforters

❖ Staying up late to watch mindless TV programmes

❖ Spending too much money in order to make up for boring work

❖ Feeling powerless

❖ Blaming others

❖ Unhelpful gossip and criticism

❖ Rushing around because time seems short

❖ Worrying about money, weight issues, housework, family

❖ Imagining negative possibilities

What am I willing to take up?

❖ Magic morning moments with my Guardian Angel

❖ Morning breathing exercises

❖ Regular meditation, twice daily for twenty minutes

❖ Daily physical exercise, for flexibility and stamina

❖ Regular quality time with loved ones

❖ Practising mindfulness during working activities

❖ Wise work, wise recreation, wise sustenance

❖ Offering silent blessings to everyone I meet

❖ Before-bed thankfulness, gratitude for abundant gifts

Now, the magic gift in this whole process is that, if you are committed to taking up the positive habits, the negative ones will begin to disappear of their own accord, without any sense of hard work, anxiety or stress. Think of yourself as the landscape designer of your life and your Guardian Angel as the head gardener, who makes sure everything comes up roses – your wish is their command! Meditation is what you do to water and feed your plants.

Exercise: Designing Your Personal Paradise

What would you like to find in your own Garden of Eden?

1. Find a very large piece of paper, such as a piece from a flip-chart pad (A1), or stick several smaller pieces together. You will also need some coloured pens or pencils.

2. Draw a large circle, as big as the paper allows. This represents the boundary of your Garden of Eden.

3. In the middle of the circle draw a tree. Make sure it has a nice, sturdy trunk. Draw seven long, strong roots going downwards and seven branches going upwards with lots of green leaves. Add seven big circles to represent fruit.

4. Now take some time to think about what you would like in your Garden in the following seven areas:
   ❖ Relationships
   ❖ Career

❖ Finance
❖ Health
❖ Wisdom
❖ Adventure
❖ Entertainment

Don't rush. You might like to draw your tree on one day, then think about your 'fruit' while you are out and about, and come back to the project the next day.

5. Fill in the fruit circles – one for each of the seven topics – with pictures (you could collect pictures from magazines for this or just draw little cartoons) or words that describe your vision of your life, if everything in your Garden was as lovely as you can imagine.

6. Now sit quietly with your picture and ask yourself: what do I need to do to nourish my tree, so that these fruits will grow big and strong? There are seven roots in your picture. Think of seven key words that represent the nourishment you need. Here are some possibilities:
❖ Confidence
❖ Love
❖ Beauty
❖ Time
❖ Stability
❖ Meditation
❖ Companionship
❖ Books
❖ Walking
❖ Good food

Use a separate piece of paper to write down as many words as possible that come into your mind, then choose the seven that seem most significant.

7. As you work through this process, you may notice some negative emotional responses. Part of you might well be feeling that some of those roots are not as strong as you would like them to be. Simply recognise those thoughts are there, but don't become bogged down in them. You can come back to your garden later after doing some other exercises, when you may develop a clearer picture of what needs to change or improve.

8. Spend a little more time with your tree picture, allowing yourself to feel any emotions, positive or negative. Then give thanks to the Universe, or God – whatever word you like to use – for giving you life and for your creative possibilities.

9. Roll up your picture, tie it with a ribbon and keep it in a safe place.

Meditation keeps your connection to the divine clear and constant

When I learned meditation in the 1970s, I started to have unexpected visions and experienced mystical states that I had only read about in spiritual literature. Over the last thirty-five years or so, I have continued with my meditation, which is a key activity in my life. I have experimented with different methods of meditation and kept records of my experiences. I have also researched other people's spiritual experiences of all kinds, both ancient and modern, including reports of angelic encounters. So, although the topic of spiritual or paranormal experience is vast and there is always more to discover, I have some clear ideas about these experiences, what they might mean and how we can encourage them for our positive benefit.

People are sometimes surprised when I say I don't believe in anything supernatural. What I *do* believe is that there are invisible layers and dimensions underlying the so-called 'everyday' reality that we experience with our usual five senses. In modern Western culture, our habit is to be mostly concerned with physical survival, so we have a tendency to live only through the five senses and rarely take notice of occurrences that do not fit into our everyday expectations. Yet all kinds of small miracles happen every day and we take them for granted. Often they are to do with the timing just being right. For example, when the postman calls *just in time* to help an old lady, living alone, who has fallen down the stairs, or you miss the train connection that would have been *just in time* for you to be involved in a major rail disaster. When you are running late for work, so your sister is *just in time* to catch you before you leave to tell you that you must drive straight to the hospital where your mother has been taken after a heart attack, giving you the opportunity to hold your mum's hand before she dies. If you decide to move house and, when you just happen to mention it to a friend, she says you are *just in time*, because she was going to let her little cottage to someone through an agency, but would much rather you rented it. Minor connections such as these are happening all the time.

Of course, some people are *just in time* to be involved in the train crash and are injured, or die. Some will arrive at the hospital *just in time* to miss the parent they wanted to make peace with, and so on. There is always a metaphysical reason for the occasions that seem to be 'bad'. Remember the three possibilities: trials, foresight or karma (see pp. 6–7).

The hidden dimensions become more accessible to us when we allow our minds to expand. Our Guardian Angel acts as our guide and keeps us safe when we ask to journey into the mysterious realms where Angels and other discarnate beings exist. But we cannot make much progress without meditation, which is the primary technique for opening our hearts and minds to the deeper layers of Creation. If we want to enter the worlds of the Angels, meditation provides the key to the Kingdom of Heaven within us.

Think of your mind as a deep ocean and your everyday consciousness as a little boat bobbing about on the surface, with you sitting in it, keen to paddle a straight line so that you don't bump into other boats or collide with anything floating around. For the most part, you don't bother to think about what happens beneath the surface of the water; you don't feel you have time to do anything except concentrate on your paddling. But there are hidden forces at work, one of which is your Guardian Angel, trying to steer you in the right direction. The ocean of your consciousness goes down for many, many fathoms and when you meditate, allowing your boat to float for a while, you will find 'deep-sea diving' brings great joy and confidence into your life. You can find yourself talking to guides and Angels, or you can sit in stillness and silence on the ocean floor, allowing the power of Divine Energy to surge through you. All the collected past and future wisdom of humanity can be accessed through meditation and, with practice and commitment, you can connect to the cosmic highways that allow you to journey to other galaxies and solar systems.

One great Jewish mystic, Abulafia (who used Raziel as his pen name, after the great Archangel Raziel, keeper of mysteries), said that we all need to unseal the 'knots' in our Soul, allowing our inner 'Gates of Light' to open. The Christian mystic, Dame Julian of Norwich, used the image of shutters at a window, telling us that all we have to do is open our shutters and God's light will pour in, like sunshine through a window. Your Guardian Angel needs you to unseal your knots, or open your shutters, clearing the way for the light to shine through you, so that you can live at 200 per cent. If you were a runner in a marathon, your supporter would be there at the staging posts with a constant supply of water; meditation is the 'H_2O' for sustaining long-distance spiritual progress. But your Guardian Angel can't meditate for you. The water fountain is waiting, but you need to drink from it.

How to meditate

Over the last thirty years or so, the word 'meditation' has become much more popular. Once, meditation was seen as something cultish, but nowadays it is recognised as a useful practice by all sorts of people, including the medical profession. You will often see posters and advertisements for the many different methods of meditation and it may be that you have never started meditating or settled on a technique, simply because you don't know where to start.

The simplest form of meditation is just to sit quietly and observe your thoughts and feelings, attempting to become a witness, detached from the activities in your own mind. This is a really challenging way to start. As a young teenager I tried a technique suggested by the teacher at the Buddhist Society. We were asked to close our eyes and visualise all our thoughts as white chalk words, written on our inner blackboard. Then we could take up our imaginary duster and clear the thoughts away, just like a school-teacher wipes the blackboard clean. I found this quite impossible. My thoughts were bouncing all over the place and I didn't get time to clean my slate before some other thoughts manifested in white chalk. I felt like Mickey Mouse as the sorcerer's apprentice in the movie *Fantasia*, trying to keep up with the buckets of water he had magically created while his boss was out of sight. The water kept coming and Mickey could never sweep it away quickly enough. But this idea might work for you, if you don't have an unruly mind!

Another method is simply to watch your breath, observing the in- and out-breaths, perhaps saying 'in' and 'out' as you inhale and exhale. This can be quite effective and easy, but it is also very relaxing and you might just drop off to sleep – I recommend doing it at night if you are restless.

I teach my students how to use a mantra, which is a simple word, usually two or three syllables long, consisting of sounds that introduce useful vibrations into your mind. Ancient sacred languages, such as Sanskrit or Hebrew, provide suitable words, with vibrations that allow you to settle into a deep state of mental and physical stillness. For example, in Sanskrit, the most famous mantra is 'aum', pronounced as two syllables – 'ow' then 'mm'. Hindu yogis consider this mantra too powerful for ordinary 'householders' – people like you and me – to use in their everyday lives. Such a sound is called 'primordial', because it resonates with sounds that occur naturally in the universe. Another primordial sound is 'sssh', which is like the noise left over from the Big Bang. This sound has been picked up on radio telescopes and is a constant background noise in our lives, even if we cannot hear it with our normal hearing. 'Ssh' and 'om' are found in the Hebrew word *shalom*, which means 'peace'; *shema* in Hebrew means 'listen'. Both these words make a good mantra and I have often used them in workshops when I introduce people to the mantra meditation method.

The mantra technique is taught in Transcendental Meditation, but it is a universal method, found in many mystical traditions, and it is quite possible for you to choose your own mantra. The poet, Alfred, Lord Tennyson, described how, as a young boy, he repeated his own name over and over until he found himself in a deep state of stillness:

> ... *when I*
> *Sat all alone, revolving in myself*
> *That word which is the symbol of myself.*
> *The mortal limit of the Self was loosed,*
> *And passed into the Nameless, as a cloud*
> *Melts into Heaven.*

> (from 'The Ancient Sage')

In one of his letters, Tennyson describes what he experienced as a 'state of transcendent wonder, associated with absolute clearness of mind'. Tennyson didn't refer to the word 'mantra' and he may have stumbled on this method by accident; there is no evidence he had knowledge of Indian mystical techniques.

If you want to try a mantra meditation, my 'Simple Meditation' technique is available on CD or as an MP3 download (see Theolyn's CDs, p. 222). For more information about meditation, see Appendix 1, or follow the instructions below.

Allow yourself plenty of quiet time for your first experiment, including before and after the meditation session itself. The day before you plan to work with your mantra for the first time, spend the evening quietly, avoid alcohol and rich foods, and give yourself a nice relaxing bath.

Treat your first session as a personal initiation and honour yourself by putting fresh flowers in your room and lighting candles. Allow yourself at least half an hour when you will not be disturbed – switch off the phone and muffle the doorbell. It is best not to meditate immediately after a meal, since your body will want to be busy digesting food, and the process of meditation encourages all the bodily functions to slow down.

Meditation: Using a Mantra

Choose a simple word, preferably of two syllables. It can have an appropriate meaning – for example, 'peaceful' – but also think carefully about its sound. Sounds that have hard consonants in them are not useful.

Having chosen your word, you can begin:

* Sit quietly in a comfortable chair that supports your spine in an upright position. Allow your hands to rest loosely in your lap. Keep your legs uncrossed and your feet squarely and firmly on the floor.

* Your actual meditation time should be fifteen to twenty minutes. Keep a clock near at hand, but don't set an alarm, unless it is absolutely necessary – in which case try to set it a good five minutes after you are supposed to finish meditating. It is not a good idea to be shocked out of a deeply relaxed state. You can peek at the clock at any time during the meditation. As you gain experience you will discover that you can set your internal clock, just as you can 'set' yourself to wake up at a certain time in the morning.

* Have a glass of spring water nearby, to sip when you have finished.

❖ Start by checking through your body and focusing your attention on any tension spots. Say to yourself, 'Relax', 'Let go', 'This is my time'.

❖ Observe your breathing. As you breathe, say to yourself, 'in', then 'out', 'in' and 'out'. Let your breathing become deeper and slower.

❖ When you have settled into a gentle rhythmical breathing pattern, say your chosen mantra quietly to yourself. Keep repeating it to yourself, over and over, but gradually allow the repetition to be in your head, so that you are no longer using your voice. After this first session, it is not necessary to say it aloud; you can start off simply thinking your mantra.

❖ After some repetitions you will probably find your mind wandering. This is quite natural; once you realise you are no longer repeating the mantra, simply start again. Don't try to force yourself into concentrating, but keep your attention on it lightly. You will notice that the mantra changes; it may slow down or speed up, or you may no longer know where it begins or ends. Then, after a while, the daily thoughts may trickle back in. When you notice them, return again to the mantra.

❖ Gradually you will notice a deep stillness coming over your whole being. You may feel a sense of expansion beyond your body, and clarity in your mind that is like a bright light. This sensation is very blissful – I usually find myself smiling when it happens. It is a timeless experience in which you understand that who you are has no beginning and no end.

❖ If this doesn't happen the first time you meditate, don't give up; your mind will eventually get the message. The most important thing is to take a light approach without aiming for mind-blowing results. Allow your meditation to be simple and easy, and accept whatever it was works for you.

❖ When your meditation time is up, gradually bring yourself back to the room by wriggling your hands and toes, shrugging your shoulders, stretching and generally shifting your body back into action. It is useful to open your eyes slowly – look at the floor at first, so that you do not have a sudden influx of visual images.

Whatever method you choose, or whatever suits you, please do meditate regularly. You will experience the most amazing joy and, by extension, you will spread more joy out into the world. Meditation is an essential tool for anyone who wants to have an intimate relationship with their Guardian Angel.

Grounding – the other half of your 200 per cent

We always have to find a good balance between our spiritual and physical lives. Meditation allows us to disengage from everyday concerns, but we must be careful to come back to Earth and re-engage. The movement between the divine and the everyday worlds will become easier as you get the hang of it, but there are several useful activities that will ensure you don't drift off into a dream state, when you should also be paying full attention to your physical life:

❖ Immediately after meditation, stretch your limbs and stamp your feet

❖ Walk daily

❖ Take regular physical exercise that you enjoy – yoga, Pilates, dance, or tai chi, for instance

❖ Do some gardening or hug trees

❖ Spend time with animals

❖ Play with children

❖ Go barefoot on grass or sand

❖ Swim, especially in the sea

❖ Do some cooking, sewing, pottery, carpentry, or other arts or crafts

When we meditate, we touch the edges of the Divine Source, then we return to the world and bring that beauty with us, but we have to find a way to express the pleasure of our experience in Creation. Creating beauty, giving love, sharing with friends and family – these are ways in which we allow the divine light to shine in the world.

Step by gentle step

These are my recommendations for developing your loving relationship with your Guardian Angel and bringing the joy you experience out into the world:

❖ Meditate twice a day, before breakfast and before supper.

❖ Talk to your Guardian Angel as you wake and when you go to bed.

❖ Send blessings and love to everyone as often as possible.

❖ Keep well grounded with physical exercise and practical activities.

6

Meeting Your Guardian Angel

... at last I came to my house
With its garden of sweet roses
And I surrendered my dusty garments,
And curled myself into the Angel's hand.

THEOLYN CORTENS

Divine dating

Before you can develop a relationship with your Guardian Angel, you need to have a sense of who or what they might be like. It's a bit like internet dating, in that at first, the person on the other end of the emails is invisible to you, but gradually you start to share experiences – favourite things, hobbies, life stories and photographs. You build up an intimate picture of someone you have never met in the flesh.

So what would your Guardian Angel be like? How would you know if you had made a real contact? Every Guardian Angel is unique, so I cannot describe yours for you, but I can suggest some clues.

Let's start by thinking about Angels in general. What *is* an Angel? An Angel is a kind of template, a hidden structure made of such fine vibrations that we cannot experience it through our usual five senses. Everything that exists in nature has an Angel that holds its shape and supports its development. The Angel for a flower is embedded in the seed and, as the flower grows, the Angel encourages the flower to unfold its beauty. Science has discovered an underlying pattern-holding system in Nature that can be measured – this is DNA. We are told that DNA is the hidden code that decides the way a living organism develops. My legs are short, my husband's legs are long – that is all because of our genetic make-up, encoded in our DNA. A poppy is red, a cornflower is blue – DNA again.

Scientists tell us there is no need to talk about Angels. A giraffe has a long neck because of natural selection, developed over time in order to reach leaves at the tops of trees. Perhaps there were no leaves left at the bottoms of the trees, because some short-necked giraffes or other creatures had eaten them all. According to science, natural selection is based on random occurrences being helpful to creatures that adapt to make the most of the opportunities, thus ensuring their survival. The DNA records the adaptation and is the mechanism for passing it on to future generations. There is no intelligence, no decision, no choice, no will – just chance.

But if the underlying power that drives life is intelligent and looks for every possibility to create beauty and harmony, then we can say that the Angel of each creature represents an inbuilt desire, not just to survive, but also to solve the problem of staying alive in the most elegant and beautiful way possible. There are so many creatures on our planet that seem to be beautiful for no good reason, we can only imagine they just *want* to be beautiful. The turning point in the DNA adventure is creative intention: the DNA does not limit the giraffe; rather, the giraffe makes choices and the changes in DNA follow the new pattern. After all, the giraffe could have scampered off to a different venue in order to find ground-level food to eat. The short-necked giraffe *wants* to grow a long neck and the animal's Angel supports and encourages its intention. Angels support poppies being red and cornflowers being blue as well.

Think of an artist who is creating a painting. Her ideas are all in her head, but as she focuses her intention on the blank canvas and the available paints, she is able to imagine how her painting will look. DNA can be likened to the artist's materials and the Angels are the artists. But remember, these Angel artists have all been commissioned by a great patron, who has unlimited resources and supervises the overall vision of the creative masterpiece. This patron is 'God', or 'Divine Intelligence' – whatever title you might like to use. So, we could say that an Angel is an idea in the mind of God, an idea focused on manifesting something that fits into a larger creation, based on harmonious ideals. But, like an artist, Angels need a palette of paints or other media in order to manifest the vision.

Guardian Angels have exactly the same task: every human being has a Guardian Angel, whose only desire is to manifest a beautiful, fully realised and powerful human being in the world. The difference between us and the giraffe is that we have a developed consciousness and can consciously collaborate in this process if we choose. We can also inhibit or block our own amazing possibilities, and this leads to personal and collective unhappiness.

So, your Guardian Angel is your inner template, guiding you towards becoming the kind of being you know you could become – one that is both fully human and fully divine. Guardian Angels need their human counterparts as collaborative partners in manifesting a world full of remarkable human beings and a world that is harmonious. Your Guardian Angel *is* the divine part of yourself – not your 'higher self', which is an aspect of your human personality, but your divinity, the God within you. And, as with internet dating, you can gradually uncover the nature of your own divinity by constantly asking questions, and by sharing your ideas, experiences, hopes and desires with your Guardian Angel. You won't be using the worldwide web, but your inner 'web', which you can access through meditation and your creative imagination.

Once you make a commitment to collaborate with your Guardian Angel, your sense of this presence will grow. Sometimes you may feel it as if someone was standing beside you, or behind you. You will notice thoughts arising that seem to come from 'somewhere else' – powerful thoughts that seem to sort out problems instantly. You will experience 'coincidences' and come across people, books or objects that seem totally perfect for you. It is like a love affair and it is not one-sided – your Guardian Angel needs you as much as you need your Guardian Angel!

Imagine your ideal Guardian Angel

Some people ask me, 'How do I know I am experiencing a real Angel and not just something I have imagined?' Our imagination is a tool that enables you to reach the wisdom that exists in the deeper layers of your consciousness and bring it into your everyday consciousness. It can make use of existing ideas that are already in your mind, images that have usually been planted there because of your cultural background. Angels are usually portrayed with white wings, long, flowing garments and beautiful hair. Sometimes, pictures of Angels are more masculine – they might wear armour, for example, and carry a sword. So, when you ask to meet your Guardian Angel, many possibilities can stir in our unconscious as a way to clothe your divine helper, who in reality has no physical form, no gender, no wings and certainly no clothing.

But you need to experience your Guardian Angel in a way that makes you feel comforted, supported, encouraged and focused on your mission or destiny. Something deep within you will make some choices and an image will start to form that makes sense to you – you will 'see' an image that represents all the qualities your Guardian Angel has to offer you. But you can also consciously *choose* how your Guardian Angel might look, whether it might be a 'he' or a 'she', for instance. And you can also consciously choose a name, especially as you develop your relationship to the stage where you are engaging in regular conversations.

The Visualisation on p. 67 takes you on a journey to meet your Guardian Angel in your own sacred building. As preparation for your journey you could try the following exercise:

1. Sit quietly with a pad of plain paper and some colours near to hand.

2. Meditate for a few moments, then open your eyes and answer the following questions as quickly as possible. Don't think about the answers – just write down the first thing that comes to mind:
    ❖ If your Guardian Angel was a physical being, would it be a 'he' or a 'she'?
    ❖ What colour skin does your Guardian Angel have?
    ❖ Does your Guardian Angel have wings? A halo?
    ❖ If not, how do you know it is an Angel?
    ❖ Does your Guardian Angel wear clothes? If so, describe them.
    ❖ Does your Guardian Angel have any equipment or other objects? Armour? Sword? Chalice?
    ❖ When your Guardian Angel speaks, what kind of voice do you hear?.

3. Now half close your eyes and breathe deeply so that you are in a semi-meditation, and make an image on the paper. Try not to guide your hand consciously, but allow it to work automatically. At first, you may feel self-conscious and think you have to try hard, but gradually, if you can achieve a peaceful state of relaxed focus, your hand will start to move, apparently of its own accord.

If you have already used the visualisation journey below (perhaps because you have read other books of mine or picked it up from one of my websites), I suggest you still take this opportunity to revisit the sacred building and talk to your Guardian Angel again. Gaining confidence in this relationship is essential if you are to make the most of the other spiritual-development exercises in this book.

Before any inner work of this kind, remember to create a space for yourself that feels safe and comfortable – an easy chair or sofa is best. (Although some people like to lie down, I think this does mean you run the risk of going to sleep.) Have a drink of water near by. Choose a time when you are unlikely to be interrupted by family, friends or pets, and you'll also need to allow plenty of time after your inner journey to write down your experiences in your Journal. Don't forget to turn off all telephones.

Visualisation: Journey to Meet Your Guardian Angel

❖ Breathe deeply and slowly, in and out, watching your breath for a couple of minutes before allowing your imagination to take you on the journey.

❖ Imagine you are in a very beautiful sitting room. You are sitting on a comfortable sofa, facing French windows that open out on to a wonderful garden. In your mind's eye, you rise from the sofa and walk over to the doors. You open them carefully and step out into the garden.

❖ You wander through the garden where the colours of the flowers and the dewy grass seem brighter than anything you have ever seen. You can smell the perfume of the flowers and the newly mown grass. You can see butterflies flitting among the blossoms. You can hear birds singing in the clear blue sky above you.

❖ As you walk slowly through the garden you come to a gate, which leads out of the garden. You open the gate and find yourself in a country lane.

❖ You walk along the lane. On one side is a hedge full of birds and little animals. On the other is a field of golden corn with brightly coloured wild flowers – poppies, daisies and cornflowers.

❖ Eventually, you come to some trees and find yourself wandering into a wood. The wood is quiet and you notice how the sun shimmers through the green and golden leaves.

❖ There is a path through the wood, marked with shining white stones. Although the trees are getting thicker, there appears to be a light ahead of you and you keep following the white stones until you come to a clearing, where the light comes from.

❖ In the clearing you find a shining building and you know that this is a sacred space, which has been waiting for you.

❖ The door of your sacred building is open and you sense that a welcome awaits you. As you walk inside, you know that you have come home. The door gently closes behind you, providing a safe haven.

❖ You are in a golden room where a seat is waiting for you. When you sit down, you feel peaceful, happy and content. This is the place where you will meet and talk with your Guardian Angel.

❖ Say in your mind: 'I now call my Guardian Angel to come to me. I would like to know your name and please tell me anything I need to know which is important to me at this stage on my life path.'

(Short silence.)

❖ Now say thank you to your Guardian Angel and get up from your seat. Move gently towards the door of your sacred room.

❖ You can still feel the presence of your Guardian Angel as the doors open gently and you step outside. You walk back down the path of white stones that guides you through the wood.

❖ Gradually, the trees begin to thin out and you can see the sun shining through the leaves. You find yourself back on the lane, with the hedge with birds and wild animals on one side of you and the swaying golden corn and wild flowers on the other.

❖ Eventually, you find the gate that leads back into the garden and you wander through it, smelling the flowers, listening to the birds singing and watching the butterflies flitting.

❖ You walk towards the house and step back through the French windows into the sitting room. Walk back to the comfortable sofa and sit down once more.

❖ Before opening your eyes, breathe deeply and stretch your body like a cat. Shrug your shoulders and wriggle your hands and feet.

❖ You may need to take some time before you open your eyes. When you do, remember to look downwards at first. Coming back into everyday reality should be a gentle process.

Spend some time recording your experience in your Journal. Archiving our experiences is is an important part of spiritual development, because it allows us to see how we are progressing.

Your Guardian Angel's name

The name of your Guardian Angel is a mystery that is known only to you. If, during the time you spent with your Guardian you did not receive a name, then this is nothing to worry about. You can wait, confidently, knowing that this name will come to you one way or another: perhaps in a dream, perhaps when you are glancing through a book that just happens to come your way. Or, you can consciously choose a name, even if you think to yourself that it is a name that 'will do for now', until another one presents itself that feels more 'right'.

I don't tell people the name of my Guardian Angel; to me, this relationship is a very private affair. Occasionally, I will mention the names of guides that have helped me, like Pythagoras, because he is available to everyone if they choose to consult him. But it is really important to remember that you, as a physical human being are in charge of your physical, human life. I often have the impression that people who like to work with guides and Angels abdicate their personal responsibilities, suggesting that because they had an inspiration from a 'higher source', that what they are doing has some special importance. Your Guardian Angel is a collaborator and whether his or her name is something 'special', like Gabriel, or something 'ordinary', like Bill, you just have to get on with your task in life. Don't fall into the glamour trap, or allow this work to be an escape from everyday practicalities and responsibilities. Better that your Guardian Angel is called 'Jim' and you make a positive difference in the world, than that he or she is called Zazaziel and you can't organise a children's tea party.

How your Guardian Angel makes its presence felt

I hope that the visualisation on p. 67 has helped you gain a sense of your divine 'other half', even if you haven't 'seen' anything or heard a name. Just asking to open this connection will initiate deep stirrings in your Soul and it is quite probable that for a few days, and perhaps while you are reading this book and doing more exercises, you will notice changes and signs. Sometimes, very small occurrences will make you think twice, like finding something you thought was lost, or someone you haven't met for ages ringing up out of the blue, just when you were thinking of them.

You might feel a presence with you while you are doing something ordinary, like washing up. Including quiet, practical tasks in your daily life will allow your Guardian to prompt you towards important things. If your life is full of chatter, with the television or CD player filling every possible gap, your Guardian won't have a chance to contact you. No wonder the mystics always preferred to live in natural surroundings, away from the social hubbub! You don't need to live in a hut in a forest in order to get in touch with your divine nature, but you should allow yourself quiet times, daily meditation and the occasional retreat.

Your Guardian will take opportunities when you offer them. When you meditate, you are seeking a place of stillness and complete silence but, on the edges of that state, the Angels and other guides can reveal themselves and give you messages. Try, if you can, to find time to meditate for twenty minutes twice a day. See if you can also spare an extra few minutes after your meditations in order to write down any messages that may have arrived when you were emerging from that deep, still silence.

Your dreaming state also gives your Guardian the chance to communicate with you, so keep a dream diary by your bed. Usually, dreams that are messages from your Guardian or other guides that want to help you are quite easy to interpret and are invariably reassuring. But always keep a note of the time when you awoke from any dream; if ever you have a really significant dream that feels very important, but you don't quite understand its meaning, you could consult an astrologer, who can help you gain insights by setting up a chart for the date, time and place of the dream.

Guardian Angel stories from my students

The people who come to my classes, or work from home using my correspondence course or eClasses, come from a wide variety of backgrounds. Some of them have had a religious upbringing and may already have ideas about Guardian Angels, learned when they were children. Even if they weren't brought up in any particular religious tradition, they will probably know something about Angels, if only from Christmas cards. Some students may have been reading recent Angel books and using some of the many Angel oracle cards published during the last few years. So their minds already have lots of visual material to work on. This means that students who receive an image of their Guardian Angel often see it looking like the classic picture of an Angel, with white wings, a luminous white gown and a golden halo.

Our imaginative forces have a strong tendency to search our mental records for some useful reference to describe what we are experiencing. As I have said already, Angels don't wear gowns and they don't literally have wings, but our minds create images in order to process the information from celestial helpers, guides, Angels and other invisible beings, in a way we can understand and will make sense to us. This is why most people do see their Guardian Angel dressed in the 'usual' style; but, on occasions, spiritual seekers are surprised because an unexpected vision appears.

PATRICIA'S STORY

Patricia had been brought up as a Roman Catholic. She did tell me after the Guardian Angel class that she had come along because her husband had died a few months earlier and she thought I might be able to bring her a message from him. However, I am not a spiritual medium, so that wasn't what happened. Patricia did my guided visualisation, 'Journey to meet your Guardian Angel' (see p. 67), and although she had never experienced an inner journey of this kind before, she had a surprise and she shared with the group what she had seen.

An Indian gentleman in a beautiful coloured silk jacket and an elaborate turban, decorated with a big brooch and a feather, had appeared in her inner vision. He smiled sweetly at her, but did not speak. Patricia was very excited by this arrival – and puzzled. She told us about her Catholic background and said that she fully expected to see her Guardian wearing the usual outfit. Why, she asked, would she see an Indian person? I explained that, when given the opportunity, our Soul will find any way it can to prompt us to look at life from a spiritual perspective, instead of basing all our decisions on purely practical concerns. 'If your Guardian Angel has appeared wearing an Indian costume,' I said, 'maybe your Soul is asking you to consider something new and unusual.'

Patricia left the class on cloud nine. She had received something very special and unexpected – not a message from her husband, but an unusual message from her Angel. She wasn't sure what it meant, but she was open to exploring the possibilities that were calling to her. Later, she got in touch with me and said she had decided, just a few days after the class, to use some of the money coming to her from her husband's will to go on a trip to India and to see what unfolded.

Kathleen Pepper, a friend and colleague who has been facilitating Angel courses for many years, is a healer at White Eagle Lodge, a well-known spiritual centre in West London. Kathleen is a very well grounded and wise teacher. Kathleen uses the title 'personal' or 'special' Angel for the Guardian Angel, and her own story just goes to show that these Angels can appear in very unlikely costumes.

KATHLEEN'S STORY

One day, when I was facilitating an Angel course, I took the participants through a visualisation to see a special Angel who would be with them to help them. I was surprised when I saw a special Angel for me as well, because I don't tune in for myself when facilitating a workshop. But there he was, very large and dressed in motorbike leathers. 'My name is Kenneth,' he said. 'I am always with you when you go out by yourself. My work is to protect you.' He was very insistent that he was not to be called Ken. I would never have imagined that an Angel of light would look like a biker, but there you are. I know I am always safe. A long time later, I asked him to show me what he is like as a heavenly Angel, an Angel of Light. He showed me that he is enormous, as tall as the room we were in. I don't visualise Angels with robes or wings. I see their light and colours and usually their eyes. His light was all shades of violet, lilac and amethyst. He is definitely an Angel of Light, working on the violet ray. If anyone noticed him with me in the city, they would see him in his biking leathers.

Guardian Angels can appear in many guises and sometimes we can only experience them as light and sound. Some people don't 'see' anything at all, but feel a warm presence, a comforting feeling, a sensation in the air around their heads or high-pitched singing. Don't be concerned if you don't experience strong visual impressions – this doesn't mean there is no one there for you. The awareness of your Guardian Angel is an interior experience and will be unique to you. But, there is one thing everyone has in common: anyone who has felt the presence of their Guardian Angel will tell you they immediately felt comforted, secure and loved.

7

Every Day in Every Way

The birthday of my life is come: my Love has come
to me

CHRISTINA ROSSETTI

Experiencing the love of your Guardian Angel

After a workshop at one of the annual Mind Body Spirit shows in London, a lady came to me with tears in her eyes. She took me by the hand and thanked me profusely for the workshop; she said that she had had such a beautiful meeting with her Guardian Angel – more beautiful than she could have imagined. 'I will never feel alone again,' she told me. I felt profoundly moved myself, because I had created a two-hour event in the middle of a busy city which had allowed something wonderful to happen for at least one participant – someone I had never met before.

When I offer workshops and courses about Angels, or write books like this one, my intention is to help people to reach deep inside themselves to discover the power and wisdom of their own divinity. The reason I look for different ways to enable this process for my students is because I have found techniques for touching those dimensions myself; I have personally experienced the wonder of the 'Kingdom of Heaven' that is hidden within each one of us. So I must admit I am 'on a mission', to encourage other people to explore that kingdom for themselves – and the first stage of the journey is a meeting with your Guardian Angel. When I am able to witness this awakening in people on courses and workshops, I feel such joy and delight. It is like being at a wedding ceremony for two people who are head over heels in love. But, like someone who offers a dating service for singles, when the magic happens and a new relationship starts to blossom, I know I am only the instrument for something amazing that wanted to happen anyway. My own role is just a tiny part of a bigger story.

However, as you should know, a fairy tale does not end with the wedding of the prince and princess. A loving relationship of any kind develops over time and, even though your Guardian Angel is the most forgiving of partners, you will only experience the depth of Divine Love if you open your inner gates. Then you can let the light of this power flow through you and out into the world. Your capacity for receiving love becomes greater when you open your heart and start to give love yourself.

In the *The Rime of the Ancient Mariner*, Samuel Taylor Coleridge describes how the mariner carries a dead albatross around his neck because he shot the bird that the other sailors believed was bringing them luck. For many days and nights the mariner suffers, surrounded by his dead comrades, alone on an endless sea without any drinking water. His sense of guilt and shame overwhelms him until, eventually, he notices some brightly coloured sea creatures darting in the water and finds himself spontaneously blessing them. As soon as he thinks the blessing, the albatross falls from his neck and he is released from his burden of guilt. This story is a beautiful illustration of the way we can be weighed down with negative thoughts about ourselves, but when we turn our attention to the beauty of the world, and to other people and creatures, extending our blessing to them, our heart opens to the power of love. We receive love as we give it.

So it is with your Guardian Angel who is constantly prompting you to give love, so that you can experience the loving presence of your divine 'other half'. There is no limitation when it comes to Divine Love – your cup will overflow.

Magic and miracles every day

Every day, the love of your Guardian Angel creates magical events, meetings and practical possibilities that can sometimes feel like miracles. The more committed you are to this wonderful relationship, the more you will become aware of countless miracles, small and large, that add up to a life brimming over with delight.

Once you start to develop your relationship with your Guardian, you will begin to notice that certain things that previously felt difficult feel a little easier, as though you had been given the magic words, 'Open sesame!' After a while, it seems as though something you think about has prompted your Guardian to negotiate a way for you to be connected to the outcome that you were hoping for. But I think it is a two-way process – your Guardian Angel prompts you to think the best things for yourself in the first place.

In Philip Pullman's story, *The Subtle Knife* (the second in the trilogy, *His Dark Materials*), one of the main characters is a girl called Lyra who consults a special gadget called an aletheometer that answers her questions about things happening at a distance. When Lyra meets a scientist called Mary Malone, who uses yarrow stalks to consult the Chinese oracle, *I Ching* (*The Book of Changes*), Mary tries to explain the trance-like state that she and Lyra need to be in to read their oracles. She quotes some lines from the poet John Keats, who said you need to be in a state of mind where you are comfortable with 'uncertainties, mysteries, doubts, without any irritable reaching after fact and reason'. Keats called this state 'negative capability', meaning that we are not interfering with the invisible processes that allow mysteries to be revealed and the best possibilities to come to us. I prefer to say 'relaxed focus', because we have not given up our intention, so the focus is still there, but we have relaxed and we allow things to unfold. Meditation is the best tool for encouraging this state of mind. While you are meditating, you can easily drop into this state. The more you meditate, the more easily you will be able to move into 'relaxed focus', even when you are not actually meditating.

Meditation – how it takes you out of time and place

Louisa is a Reiki master who joined the Shefa training programme. When I teach people Shefa One I always send them a copy of my *Simple Meditation* CD (see Theolyn's CDs, p. 222) a couple of weeks before the workshop, so that they have the chance to start meditating using the mantra method, which I find is the most successful technique for helping people get into the deep, quiet space inside. At the beginning of the Shefa One weekend I always ask students to report their experiences and share how they got on with the mantra. Louisa was very excited. She explained that she had chosen to do the Shefa workshop because she had been using a pack of cards that I publish, called *The Angels Script*. The cards include a series of ancient symbols, for which I had channelled inspirational messages in 1996 (see www.soulschool.co.uk where you can access free readings). Louise felt the symbols were calling to her and had wondered whether this meant that she had come across them in a previous life. So she was delighted to get a chance to work with me and use the Shefa symbols as well. These aren't published for the general market; a few are on the Shefa website, and anyone tracking the history of the symbols could find references to them in old books about Kabbalah or Angels, but Louisa had only seen the symbols that appear on the Shefa website and leaflet – altogether she had seen a total of just five symbols out of the full set of twenty-two.

LOUISA'S STORY

When Louisa started to use the *Simple Meditation* mantra (which is a Hebrew sound), she quickly discovered that her mind would settle down to a state of peace and amazing calm, such as she had not experienced before; her body would feel still and completely relaxed, free of all the usual tensions. These are regular experiences for regular meditators.

Then, a few days after starting her twice-daily meditation routine, at the stage when she had increased from ten minutes each time to twenty, Louisa had an unexpected experience. She heard singing and chanting in a language she didn't know. She thought it might be Hebrew, but there was no way she could be sure. The singing was very high, and sometimes the notes seemed to disappear because her mind could not cope with the high vibrations. Although Louisa was in a completely still and passive mental state, part of her wondered inwardly whether what she was hearing was Angels singing. The answer came to her as an inner vision. She saw a clear, dark blue sky. There were no clouds, no stars, nothing.

Then, suddenly, golden letters started to appear on the blue background, as though an invisible hand was writing a message for her. The letters were like the symbols from *The Angels Script* pack – which Louise knew quite well – but there were also symbols she hadn't seen before. After a while, the writing and the singing faded; when Louisa gradually came back to her everyday state of mind, she started to draw the symbols that she could remember.

She showed the Shefa group and me her Journal and I confirmed that she had seen symbols that we use in Shefa, even though she was not consciously aware where she could have seen them before.

Meditation is not just for relaxing or even for clearing the clutter from our minds – although, obviously, it is a very important and useful tool for both. It allows us access to realms of consciousness that we are not normally aware of. During meditation we can go beyond our present moment in time and place, travelling in our spiritual state to other dimensions where we can gain wisdom and knowledge – the kind of knowledge that rarely appears in books.

Channelling messages from your Guardian Angel

Now that you have experienced the journey to your own sacred space, where you can consult with your Guardian Angel, you can choose to go there at any time when you need advice or to increase your sense that your companion is always there for you. You can also create opportunities for messages to come to you from your Guardian and there are several options open to you.

One way is to use a dowsing pendulum. If you haven't used a pendulum before, you will find a teaching video on my website (see Theolyn's websites, p. 222). My friend Lauren D'Silva offers some useful guidelines for anyone starting to dowse on the BellaOnline website (see Recommended websites, p. 224). Practise dowsing until you feel confident and, if you find you like this method, you can use it for having a conversation with your Guardian Angel. The technique allows you to receive yes or no answers very quickly, but it is not a substitute for a cosy chat with your Guardian Angel in the quiet privacy of your sacred space – it's more like sending a text message from your mobile phone. As such, dowsing is good for making decisions about travel, purchasing health supplements, knowing what to include in your diet and other practical, everyday matters. I would not, however, use a pendulum to make a life decision, such as a career change, a relationship problem or moving house.

As I mentioned earlier, you can keep a dream diary. I advise everyone to keep one. Even if you think that you never recall your dreams, you are likely to find that your dreams do become more significant while you are working through this book and, if you continue meditating, your dreams will provide useful information.

You can also keep an Angel message book – a notebook dedicated to writing messages that arrive from time to time. I have often found I receive these while I am doing something simple, like washing up. I hated this chore when I was a teenager and had lots of rows with my family when I resisted the call to the sink, but nowadays I welcome it as an opportunity to allow part of my mind to go into 'relaxed focus'. In this way, musing while doing something practical with my hands, I have not only received personal messages, but I have also had inspirations for beautiful poems that seem to come from 'somewhere else', arriving almost complete in my mind. The poet and artist, William Blake, who created so many wonderful angelic images, was an engraver. He said that this repetitive work allowed his mind to journey to other worlds. So, cooking, gardening, embroidery, crochet, and knitting – any of these activities will allow part of you to move into that quiet space where your Guardian can drop by with messages. The same Angel message book can be kept near by when you meditate.

How to recognise and trust the messages from your Guardian Angel

People often ask me how they can differentiate between a 'real' message and ideas that are 'wishful thinking'. My own experience is that messages that come from a deep state of knowing have a very different quality to them. This quality is very hard to convey, but it is a bit like the difference between real, homemade wholemeal bread, straight from the oven, and sliced brown bread that you buy in a plastic bag in the supermarket. Both are bread, but there is just more richness and comfort in the homemade version.

Sometimes, you might receive a message that just doesn't seem sensible, guiding you to do something that friends and family might think is very strange or 'out of order', in the context of the usual way things are done in your 'tribe'. Thirty-six years ago I met Will, my husband and creative partner. I was thirty years old, a single mother with two children, and he was eighteen. Just before this meeting, I had received a message from my Guardian Angel that, after ten years alone, I would meet someone and we would be married. Very soon after we met, we both 'knew' that we had to marry, even though it went against 'common sense' and, naturally, this infuriated Will's mum. I was not her favourite person for quite a while, although we are very good friends nowadays. (I should add that Will says he knew we would spend our lives together as soon as he saw me.)

If you want reassurance and advice to back up your inner promptings, it may be helpful to consult an astrologer or a reliable card reader. Although reading cards or your own horoscope yourself can be useful, somebody else can help you to see things you may otherwise miss. However, the more you communicate with your Guardian Angel and learn to trust the small confirmers that naturally develop, the less anxious you will be about whether or not your inner promptings are reliable. *Trust* is the key word here – and that comes from experience, which sometimes includes taking risks.

Cosmic ordering

In recent years, books like *The Secret, Ask and It Is Given,* and *The Cosmic Ordering Service* (see Recommended books, p. 223) have encouraged people to identify what they need and wish for – to write it down, or create a 'vision board' with pictures illustrating their aspirations. Critics have suggested that these books concentrate too much on the acquisition of material possessions and money, and not enough on quality of life, spirituality and relationships. Whatever you may feel about this, the most important thing about these books is that they remind us that our thoughts create our reality. When we think positively we set up vibrations that attract positive events, such as wealth and good health. Negative thoughts create the opposite!

Try asking your Guardian Angel to be your messenger, taking your cosmic order to the best and most efficient department to fulfil your desire. Make small requests at first, asking for things that are not very important to you, so you will let go of anxiety or attachment to the outcome. Perhaps you are keen to lay your hands on a particular book and would really like to buy a second-hand copy. This is exactly what happened to me not long ago and here's my story:

MR BENN'S MYSTERIOUS SHOP

When my children were young, we used to watch a television programme called *Mr Benn*, about a dear little man with a bowler hat who visited a fancy-dress shop where he could dress up and go on a magical journey. My eldest daughter, now in her forties, has nicknamed our local charity shop 'Mr Benn's Magic Shop', because she invariably finds exactly what she has been looking for, especially in their book section. So, when I mentioned to Will that I was going to reread Philip Pullman's *His Dark Materials* trilogy, but that my copy of the first book, *Northern Lights*, was missing from my collection, he said, 'Why don't you try Mr Benn's?'

I put the idea to the back of my mind, but the next day I did wander over to the shop, just for a browse. Then I remembered about the book and drifted into the back of the shop where the books are kept. There are hundreds of paperbacks on many shelves and they are not in alphabetical order. I skimmed a few shelves, decided I would give up and started to walk out. Then, for some unknown reason, I turned back. I glanced at another shelf and spotted a book called *Rebecca's Tale*, a modern follow-up to Daphne du Maurier's famous story, *Rebecca*. It had good reviews on the back and I thought, Right, this will keep me going. Then, somehow, my eye was drawn to the left slightly and there it was, *Northern Lights*! The title was not in big, bold lettering and the cover was quite dark and not very noticeable. I laughed out loud and had to explain myself to the lady behind the counter – although I didn't tell her we call the shop Mr Benn's!

The thing about a 'cosmic order' as small as a paperback is that we don't have a great attachment to it. After all, I could have looked on Amazon and would probably have found a cheap second-hand copy, paid online and waited for it to be delivered to my home, so it wasn't important for me to be able to buy it from a charity shop. The trick is to be able to leave orders for much more meaningful things and to treat them just as lightly as you might a second-hand paperback. Asking your Guardian Angel to take your order out into the Universe allows you to surrender the problem of finding and getting what is needed. Then a mysterious process begins, one that goes on behind every 'coincidence' and synchronicity, which involves so many layers of activity, it is almost impossible to compute with our everyday minds. Christel Nani, author of *Sacred Choices* (see Recommended books, p. 223), uses the expression 'synchrodivinity' instead of 'synchronicity', because, as she says, it is the invisible field of 'God', or 'Divine Source', that promotes these magical happenings.

Why don't you try putting in a cosmic order now? List three small things you would like to have or experience during the coming seven days. Choose things that are a bit unusual, not likely to turn up in the usual way, but also let them be things that you are not attached to. Here are some suggestions:

❖ Something that would be useful in the home. For example, you might have a gap that would be nicely filled with a bookshelf or other small piece of furniture. Measure up the space and note this in your Journal, mentioning any other qualities, such as its colour or what it's made of. Maybe you will want to paint it, so you might decide it doesn't have to have a good finish; if you decided it needed to have drawers, you might say you could add new handles, but the drawers must slide well. Be as accurate as you can, while at the same time being open to different possibilities.

❖ A book or other object that would make your life more fun. We had a plan to turn our loft room into a home cinema. We had looked on the internet and priced up a projector and a screen. We realised we might have to spend a lot of money – the screen would come in at £100 at least. So we put the project on the back burner for a while, knowing that it would come to fruition at some point, but that there were more important things to spend money on at the time. Guess what? Yes, Mr Benn turned up trumps again! We spotted a second-hand screen there, good as new, for only £4 and just the right size!

❖ Wanting to contact someone or to come across a new social activity would be good choices. Perhaps there is someone you have lost touch with. Ask your Guardian Angel to help you find this person, somehow. Or maybe you want to link up with like-minded people to meet and share ideas and experiences with. Again, your Guardian Angel can help set this up – sometimes you will suddenly have a bright idea, apparently from nowhere, that sends you off on a trail leading to a solution.

It is said that positive events and manifestations 'favour the pre-pared mind', which means that your inner state needs to be clear, receptive and open to new possibilities. Regular meditation is an essential tool for preparing the mind. However, there are additional exercises and processes that we can undertake which will speed up the changes we are looking for. These include researching the choices we made before we were born, and clearing our minds and hearts of old garbage. And in Part Two, that's just what we will be doing – read on, and I will take you, step by step, towards a clear mind that is able to make powerful choices, as well as a loving heart that is open to giving and receiving abundance.

PART TWO

*A Clear Mind and
a Loving Heart*

8

A New Way to Live

He whose face gives no light, will never become a
star.

WILLIAM BLAKE

Every human being has the capacity for spiritual realisation

What does it mean, to be 'spiritually realised'? It doesn't mean to
live in a state of total bliss so that we are unable to function at a
practical level, but to live our lives with spiritual awareness, while at
the same time dealing with the ordinary, everyday matters.
Sometimes the expression 'enlightened' is used, and one old Zen
saying explains that before enlightenment we chop wood and carry
water, and *after* enlightenment we also chop wood and carry water!
What we do, when we are spiritually realised, doesn't necessarily
change, since we are still living in a physical body and need to deal
with the necessities of living, but how we do it, how we feel about
it, and how we relate to the world does change.

The expression to be 'enlightened' suggests that we will feel lighter, since we will no longer be attached to our everyday cares and anxieties – we will see them in a new 'light'. But this new state of being is also accompanied by an inner radiance and a sense of clarity which allows us to love the world more easily, even when people and events around us may appear difficult.

'Light' is used as a metaphor in spiritual literature, to show that confusion and desperation, associated with darkness, have been dissolved. But when we reach the deepest place of stillness and silence during meditation there is often a sense of expansion, accompanied by bright light, like sunshine, which floods the mind and the body. So being 'enlightened' is not just a metaphor, we will experience the light inside us – the light of Divine Energy.

Shining with Divine Light

We all have the capacity to shine with Divine Light in the world. Throughout history, spiritual teachers, holy mystics and gurus have dedicated themselves to sharing their wisdom and knowledge with the rest of humanity. Their mission, whether Christian, Buddhist, Hindu, Jewish or Muslim, has always been founded on a common belief, that human beings could be so much happier than they are and that the potential joy they miss out on would lead to more harmony among people and more abundance in their lives.

From a spiritual perspective, the happiness that is our birthright has nothing to do with material concerns; it is not just a question of reorganising the economic status quo so that more people have a fair share of resources. The material issues, according to a spiritual view, only sort themselves out when humans realise their divine origin. We are all physical creatures and we need food, shelter and clothing, but we are also divine beings and, if we lose touch with that part of ourselves, then all the money and possessions we could imagine will not bring us joy. However, when we recognise our divine selves, we do not have to give up material comforts. The Divine Source – God, or whatever name you choose – is not puritanical, only giving out as much as we absolutely need. Not at all – Divine Energy and love are boundless! When we are fully realised, we can live a 200 per cent life (see p. 47) and have no anxieties about our material wellbeing.

Some religious traditions suggest that there is a limit to the number of people who will be 'saved', but it seems to me that we *all* have the choice. We can choose to focus our lives on self-realisation, living to our highest potential as material *and* divine beings, or just bumble along from day to day until the Angel of Death arrives and we wonder what we did with our time. (It is only because so many human beings do waste their time that this Angel is regarded as an unwelcome intruder.) Whatever one human being has achieved, we can all aspire to: once a person has run a four-minute mile, then other runners can do the same; if one human being can achieve cosmic consciousness, then we must all be able to reach this.

In times gone by, people who wanted to dedicate their lives to the sacred journey tended to retreat into caves or monasteries. But many teachers and gurus who brought spiritual teachings to the general public during the late twentieth century have agreed that we are able to incorporate spiritual practices, such as meditation and yoga, into everyday life. It is true that when we start meditation, adapting our usual stress-filled lifestyles so that we can enjoy life properly, we may find that our everyday choices – about career, diet, recreation, etc. – will change dramatically. We don't have to deliberately control our addictions, but we will find that some activities that used to fill the hours may start to feel meaningless. For instance, time spent in front of the television could be replaced by an enjoyable evening class; consuming unnecessary quantities of fast food or alcohol will not feel as satisfying as stretching your body or delighting in walking or dancing – and these changes won't have to be forced. Gradually shifting your attention to your divine qualities will allow a new balance to ease its way into your life with no real effort on your part.

We can all do this and the more people who start, the more will be drawn in that direction. But if everyone has the capacity to learn to play the piano, the person who diligently practises their scales is the one who will shine as a star. Similarly, your meditation is the equivalent of practising scales, your Guardian Angel being your piano teacher! Think about the different kinds of music that people can create; imagine what different kinds of piano teachers there would be in order for a wide variety of music to manifest. Your 'music' is the joy of life you bring into the world. When you know your Guardian Angel intimately, you will know exactly what kind of joy your heart desires to make, what you would like to bring into the world as your unique contribution to the history of humanity. Some stars in our galaxy are more noticeable than others, but there are millions of them, all giving light, and we could not do without a single one of them. So, even if you have no desire to be one of the more glamorous stars, your choice to bring your own individual light into the world will certainly mean you will shine brightly. And every shining star counts towards the glory of Creation.

Your Divine Mentor across many lifetimes

In *The Republic*, Plato explains how the human Soul makes a choice about its life and then chooses a *daimon*, or guiding spirit, to accompany it on its life journey. This version of our relationship with our Guardian Angel suggests that every time we visit Earth for a new life, we choose a new Guardian. But my own experiences have convinced me that the same Guardian Angel has been with me for many lifetimes.

From the beginning of its development our Soul has its own individual mission and will seek out possibilities for achieving that mission. Not all of those possibilities will be on Earth, for we may learn and develop in other dimensions, without being physically incarnated. But development as a fully realised, 200 per cent Earthling is the highest goal we can focus on – at least for the time being. Since our mission has a single focus, I am sure that our Guardian Angel will stay with us throughout the many incarnations we will choose. We will certainly have different guides as we proceed, because we are able to call on spiritual masters, ancestors, power animals and even extraterrestrials to give us pointers for our journey, but our Guardian Angel will be a constant point of reference, always reminding us of our overarching goal. We can also call on Archangels and other celestial beings, depending on our Soul's choices. I will be talking about celestial support more in Chapter 14.

We learn from many spiritual traditions that the Soul's journey is rarely without pitfalls. There is a paradox involved: as soon as you think you are making good progress, you are likely to fall flat on your face. On the front of Bath Abbey in England, the mediaeval stonemasons carved images of humans climbing a ladder; as the seekers approach the top, they are depicted with wings – they have transformed themselves into Angels. We can see our spiritual growth as a journey up the rungs of a ladder, but what is it that pulls us back? Traditional Christianity believes there are seven 'Deadly Sins' that humans can fall prey to: wrath, pride, lust, envy, avarice, sloth and gluttony. Many Christians also believe there are wicked spirits, always lying in wait and hoping to trap us into misbehaving. After all, the 'Devil' wants to fill his kingdom with 'fallen' souls! Sometimes these tricksters, leading us to temptation, are depicted as snakes.

The old children's board game of Snakes and Ladders – in which you move your counter across the board towards the finish, moving up when you land on a ladder, but back down if you land on a snake – was originally used as a spiritual teaching tool. It was intended to encourage people to keep their attention on their Soul's purpose to reconnect with their divinity and not be dismayed by setbacks. In this book, I will be sharing inspirations and stories designed to support you when climbing your spiritual ladder and giving you some techniques for dealing with the snakes, although I must add that snakes are not always 'baddies': they are associated with wisdom and every slide down one is a spiritual lesson.

Bringing divine wisdom into your everyday life

Everyday life presents us with a continual series of challenges, some easy to deal with and some very tough. We have an instinct to try to make things easy for ourselves, to create a perfect lifestyle, surrounded by joyous, loving people, yet it rarely seems to be that comfortable. We may wish for a Paradise to live in, but part of us knows that we need to face challenges in order to grow. Adam and Eve had to leave the Garden of Eden so that they could become fully fledged, grown-up people. Had they stayed within the garden walls they would have remained like children who had never left their playpen. Religious writer G. K. Chesterton suggested that we can come to Paradise by way of Kensal Green (in west London), while the Maharishi said it is possible to be enlightened anywhere, even if you are standing in Piccadilly Circus. The poet Wordsworth described transcendental moments that he experienced while standing in two very different places in England. He wrote this after an experience in a beautiful landscape, above the ruins of Tintern Abbey in the Wye Valley in Wales:

I have felt a presence that disturbs me with the joy of elevated thoughts.

But he also wrote a poem about an ecstatic vision he had when travelling in London, when the city was just as busy and dirty as it is now:

Earth has not anything to show more fair
Dull would he be of soul who could pass by
A sight so touching in its majesty:
This City now doth like a garment wear
The beauty of the morning;

(Composed upon Westminster Bridge. September 3, 1802)

And my husband Will describes here how he experienced glory in Paddington Station:

WILL'S EXPERIENCE

Some years ago, when we were living in Oxford, I took part in an intensive self-development weekend, run by Landmark Forum. It meant I would have to sleep on a sofa in London, in between spending very long days in a large hotel room with a hundred other students. My time was crammed from early in the morning until late at night, while I took part in exercises designed to make me question my very being. Although it had powerful spiritual implications, it was primarily designed as an extended mental exercise, though it was challenging in the extreme. There was zero tolerance over lateness and all my hours seemed to be filled with alternately processing new information and digging up old bits of mental junk that had been gathering dust in my psyche. I barely had time for eating and other everyday concerns. It was exhausting, exhilarating and an emotional rollercoaster ride.

After the course had finished, I set off for Oxford. During the early evening of Sunday, I found myself sitting in Paddington Station, killing time until my train arrived. I was relaxed, though a little tired. I was generally mulling over the events of the previous few days, but not thinking too hard. My mind was simply floating around, enjoying the sensation of not having to work. The station was busy with people scurrying around in the usual frantic way. Announcements blared, service trucks honked and drunks yelled. Then, suddenly, my vision completely changed.

Ask me what precisely changed and I find it hard to describe, but it was if the lights had suddenly come on and I was able to see everything as it 'really' was. Colours, shapes, tiny details of clothing and vast arcs in the station architecture all appeared with equal emphasis in my sight, and they were free of any value I might place on them: they simply were what they were and that was fine. In the same way, sounds entered my ears as if for the first time – I knew what they were but I heard them in a completely fresh way, rather like the famous hymn that includes the lines, 'Morning has broken, like the first morning, blackbird has spoken like the first bird ...' I have since wondered if this is what it's like to be a baby, with no preconceptions about how things 'ought' to sound or look.

My relationship with time also altered: time continued to pass, although I couldn't say whether it was passing at the usual speed (perhaps *all* speeds); simultaneously, I felt as if I was in a timeless zone, with no distinction made between one moment and the next. It therefore seems a bit strange to say that the 'next' thing happened 'later', although that's the only way I can express it here. Be that as it may, at some stage 'after' seeing and hearing everything around me in this remarkable way, the people running around in front of me lost all of their power to affect me in the way they usually do. I had no need to judge or assume anything about them – they were just living their lives in the way they thought best. This realisation, together with the experience of blithe acceptance of the world *as it is*, filled me with a huge feeling of compassion and I wept tears of joy.

These feelings of bliss passed after an indeterminate time – it could have been seconds or hours, although fortunately I didn't miss my train! – but they have remained as a powerful reminder of the reality of God; that God is not to be *believed* in, but is a tangible presence with a personal interest in me and the worlds I inhabit.

The glory of the Divine Source radiates through everything – train stations, shopping malls, supermarkets, as well as forests, lakes, mountains, fjords and deserts. In natural environments it can feel easier to let go of our usual stressed way of being, and then we are more likely to experience the wonder of Creation. When it comes to more mundane scenarios, we are invariably focused on our daily busy-ness and do not allow ourselves the time to stop and wonder. It is quite likely that people who work on the land rarely experience mystical moments, because they are going about their daily tasks and see the countryside as a place of hard work and, especially in winter, of discomfort. But the more we meditate, the more we begin to see the world through a new pair of lenses; not through 'rose-tinted spectacles', which distort reality and create a fantasy world, but through windows where the shutters have been opened, allowing the sun to pour in. We see the world in a new light, and the light shines through us, so the world in turn sees us shining like stars.

Our Guardian Angel wants to unlock the light trapped inside us and guides us in the direction of opportunities that will help us turn towards the light. Sometimes these opportunities will be very tough challenges, but if we remember that every challenge has a gift, even if the wrapping seems unattractive, then we can face our trials with grace. When we learn to stop complaining and blaming the world because things seem 'unfair', the light floods into our lives and we experience dramatic changes. Often, we will gain a new perspective on difficult events or relationships and everything takes a turn for the better. Our Guardian Angel will be cheering us all the way!

Noticing the Angel in those around you

Most people find their relationships to be highly exacting challenges. The family is a notorious hotbed for difficult interpersonal relationships. There is an old saying, 'You can choose your friends but you can't choose your family.' However, according to metaphysical principles, we *do* choose our family, seeking out learning opportunities in which we may meet up with Souls from previous incarnations, in order to resolve unfinished business, whether positive or negative. The workplace can also be chosen as a 'classroom', where you will deal with particular issues that your Soul needs to encounter. This is especially true of institutions where people stay for a long period, often building a sense of family or tribe with colleagues. The most important thing to remember is that people you encounter in your everyday life, whether family, work colleagues, the bus driver or the woman who runs the corner shop, all have Guardian Angels who want *them* to see the light. So take any opportunity you have to look for the Angels who are hovering around other people. Then you are much more likely to feel your heart open towards them, allowing you both to experience the free flow of love and joy.

Here is a simple experiment that you can conduct over the next few days:

❖ This week, on your way to and from work (as long as you are not driving), or during your lunch breaks, consciously choose to watch what is going on around you without making any judgements.

❖ Each time you notice part of your mind making comments, whether positive or negative, move your thoughts back to simple observation. Just be with what you see, as though you have no previous understanding of what it all might mean. Being with your own breath, even though there are crowds of people around, can help you become still, even in a busy environment.

❖ When you find yourself in this gentle state of non-judgement, allow yourself the privilege of looking for the light that accompanies every human being – young or old, fat or thin, beautiful or ugly, gracious or grumpy.

❖ See if you can notice the angelic aura that surrounds every individual who is sitting on the bus with you or bustling in the crowd. The poet Francis Thompson said that Jacob's ladder is 'pitched between Heaven and Charing Cross.' The mystic can see shining Angels everywhere, even in a busy city.

The reason I always encourage people to meditate is because the experience of deep stillness in meditation provides an inner foundation, from which you can more easily move into the 'now' when you are in everyday, non-meditating awareness. I also recommend Eckhart Tolle's book, *The Power of Now* (see Recommended books, p. 223), which provides great insights into achieving the altered state of consciousness that Will described (see p. 95), and would be very helpful if you find this challenging. Do you remember those 'Magic Eye' pictures that were so popular a few years ago? The images are created from a series of repeating horizontal patterns that don't seem to make a recognisable picture at first. But if you gaze at the two dimensional patterns and diverge your eyes, so that you are glancing at the patterns, rather than looking hard at them, you suddenly see a three dimensional picture that is very realistic. You could look at Magic Eye pictures time and time again, and still not 'get' the hidden image. Well, this state of being is similar – *not* trying is the best way to get there.

9

Your Divine Contract

He saw, within the moonlight in his room,
Making it rich, and like a lily in bloom,
An Angel writing in a book of gold ...

'What writest thou?' The Vision raised its head,
And with a look made all of sweet accord
Answered, 'The names of those who love the Lord.'

LEIGH HUNT

Our birth is a sleep and a forgetting

Many spiritual traditions and myths describe how our Soul chooses its new life before incarnating. The Greek philosopher Plato's version of this tradition tells us that our Soul realises it will soon forget what it has chosen and asks its *daimon,* or guardian spirit, for ongoing support. The next exercise and visualisation are designed to help you recall your choices before birth.

Just because these choices are described as a 'Divine Contract' doesn't mean to say that everyone has promised to become a saint. We all have a variety of possibilities that we can choose to develop so that we can move towards our full potential (which means to live as 100 per cent divine and 100 per cent human at the same time). We may not achieve this in one lifetime. When our Soul makes its pre-birth choices, it will have recollection of the success or failures during previous lives.

Although we may choose to arrive with specific gifts or talents, such as musical, artistic or communication skills, probably acquired during previous lifetimes, the Divine Contract does not necessarily involve a specific vocation. The possibilities we want to develop are qualities such as:

❖ Empathy

❖ Dedication

❖ Creativity

❖ Compassion

❖ Assertiveness

❖ Leadership

❖ Discernment

❖ Generosity

These qualities can be nurtured and developed in many different ways: you don't have to go into the armed forces to become a leader, although you could choose that route and, before your birth, you would probably look out for a family that would support you. If you chose to develop compassion in this life, there could be many possible vocations that would allow you to progress. Creativity can also be developed in many professions, not just in the arts and so on.

One of the problems for us when we make our pre-birth choices is that we are not necessarily able to understand all the choices that have been made by the other people we have chosen to meet. For example, a Soul that chose to be born as the son of a soldier might be disappointed when, after a few years on Earth, his father became a pacifist! Just because my Soul spotted two lovely people meeting in Westminster Abbey, it could not be guaranteed that they would give me a spiritual upbringing, so I had a long journey before I realised what my choice had been and I had to discover my own spiritual path.

Exercise: Your Choices Before Birth

Here is a short questionnaire that will help you think about the choices you made before you were born. Write the answers in your Journal.

1. Do you recall any particular moments when you were small that made you feel something was just right for you? For example, perhaps an aunt or uncle gave you a book or a gift that made something inside you go 'ping', as though a magic button had been pressed. Think back as far as you can.

2. Do you recall any subjects or activities at school that made you feel as though you could easily be good at them, as though they were already familiar to you?

3. Do you remember feeling really frustrated or angry because you weren't able to do something that felt important to you?

4. When you were young, did you have any visions or dreams for your future that you put to one side, perhaps because parents, teachers or general social pressure made you feel you could not realise

them? Did people tell you to be 'sensible' when you really wanted to follow your own heart?

5. Do you recall meeting anyone and feeling you already knew them? This could be at any age, from when you were very small to the present day.

6. Do you remember making an important life choice when you experienced a sense of being at a crossroads and part of you deep down knew that the decision would make a big impact on the rest of your life? Perhaps this was accompanied by anxiety. Try to remember what you based your choice on – intuition or your logic?

Visualisation: Remembering Your Divine Contract

❖ Remember the earlier journey you made, from the sitting room, through the garden, along the country lane and into the quiet wood, where you found that beautiful building, your own sacred space.

❖ As you breathe deeply and slowly, allow your mind to wander back there.

(Short silence.)

❖ You can see the light shining from that special room where your Guardian is waiting for you. The doors have opened, waiting to welcome you in and, as you enter, you feel that amazing sense of comfort, as though you have come home and found your beloved waiting for you. After you move into the room, the doors close gently behind you.

❖ You feel comforted, but also quite excited, because you know that something very special is going to be revealed to you.

❖ You recognise the seat from your earlier visit and sit down on it. As you do so, you notice a change in the atmosphere around you. Your Guardian Angel has come closer to you and you can feel the warmth and loving sensations that signal the presence of your Beloved.

❖ In your heart, you can now ask your Guardian Angel to help you uncover your purpose in life, the Divine Contract that you made together before you came into this life.

❖ Your Guardian encourages you to move from your seat and walk across your beautiful room towards a shining staircase that goes up through the ceiling. You stand at the bottom of the staircase and gaze upwards through the opening in the roof. You can see a blue sky that is almost cloudless. Where there are a few clouds they seem like Angels' feathers and you can hear beautiful singing, like a heavenly choir.

❖ Your Guardian Angel draws you up on to the first step and then the staircase moves like an escalator, so you find yourself going up without any effort. You pass through the blue skies, catching a glimpse of baby Angels hiding among the feathery clouds. The magical singing makes you feel as though your body is melting away.

❖ You find yourself on a cloud that seems to be the landing for the staircase. A golden light streams from the cloud and you can still hear the singing.

❖ A beautiful voice asks: 'Why you have come?'

❖ The voice knows your name and always addresses you personally. And you answer: 'I want to understand the contract that I made before I was born in my present life.'

❖ The voice replies: 'Be still, watch and all will be revealed.'

❖ As you gaze into the skies, lit up with golden rays, you see a scroll in a shining vase. The vase is made of fine material, almost transparent, like alabaster. Carved into the vase is your name – not your family name, but your own first name, the name you were given as a baby, even if you no longer use it.

❖ 'Read the scroll,' says the voice.

❖ The vase comes towards you and you are able to reach it and draw out the scroll, which has beautiful writing on it. But the letters and words do not seem to be in your own language and you feel frustrated because you cannot read them.

❖ 'All will be revealed,' says the voice.

❖ As you gaze at the words, even though you can't read them, thoughts and memories start to arise in your mind.

❖ You remember standing on that cloud a long time ago. Your Guardian Angel was with you as a powerful supporter, reassuring you that it would be good to go back to Earth as a new baby.

❖ You remember being nervous because you did not want to leave your Guardian Angel, but he or she insisted that you would never be alone.

❖ You remember that your Guardian asked you to make an agreement, a promise to make the most of your new life, and you were offered some particular possibilities, gifts or talents that would be available to you.

❖ Now spend some time with that memory, allowing the information to come back to you, either as words or pictures. As you search for those possibilities, gifts or talents in your memory, see if you can remember looking down from that cloud and imagining how wonderful your new life was going to be.

(Short silence.)

 Now, look more closely at the life you were agreeing to live. Look for the people who would be in it, the ones you hoped to meet, the ones who would support you in bringing out your possibilities.

(Short silence.)

❖ Now look again at the scroll that is your Divine Contract. Some of the words are still unclear to you, but you can see that you have written your name on it, agreeing to make the most of the life you have been offered. You realise that you made a commitment to take on the challenges life offers with good grace and that, even though your life would not be perfect, you would never lose faith in the loving support of your Guardian Angel.

❖ The beautiful voice speaks again: 'It is time to go back now.'

❖ The scroll rolls itself back into the alabaster-like vase which then seems to melt away into the golden light surrounding the cloud.

❖ You can feel your Guardian Angel's wings surrounding you and you find yourself lifted back on to the shining staircase, which moves you slowly down, down, down, through the blue skies, past the singing Angels, back towards the open roof of your sacred building.

❖ You notice your feet touching the floor and you are being guided towards the doors that open smoothly in front of you, so that you can step out into the wood again. You walk back along the path of shining white pebbles until you are back on the country lane that leads to your garden and back to the sitting room.

106

Many of my students find this visualisation takes them to a place where they feel supported by other spiritual beings, as well as their Guardian Angel, but they don't always get a very clear picture of what their Divine Contract might be. In the same way that some people find it takes time to get a clear sense of their Guardian as a presence they can rely on, I often receive reports that the request to uncover the pre-birth contract also seems a bit hard to define.

Marie, a Reiki teacher who runs her own classes and has done a lot of inner work before coming on my Guardian Angel eClass, reported that she felt she could not access all the information at once. She was told that it would be 'downloaded' gradually during meditations, as and when she needed to know. Marie explained that she always wondered why she was living in a valley in Wales – beautiful, but often very damp – when her longing was for high peaks and snowy alpine views. During the Divine Contract visualisation, Marie could see a 'slide show' that reminded her of all the classes and friendships that she had experienced in Wales, and realised that she is living in the right place, meeting the right people at the right time. 'This is a big relief!' she said.

Another student, Lorna, who works as a doctor in a general practice, said she found the Divine Contract visualisation helped her see how everything in her life ties together. She could see an overview of her life path unfolding. Lorna completed a Diploma course with me during a period while she was developing her career and having to deal with a difficult divorce at the same time. She recognised how she had the resources she needed as a single mother – childcare, friends and more.

The magnet of your Soul's desire

Your Divine Contract is a kind of inner code, a series of possibilities that you are born with. This doesn't mean you are predestined to do certain things, with no freedom of choice. In fact, we are all creating our lives as we go along from day to day. But it does mean that you have within you the potential to develop your in-born talents as best you can. Outer circumstances may seem to help or hinder our progress in life, and it is true we may be influenced by national or personal events, as well as other people. However, when we are truly focused, we create our own circumstances and attract what we need towards us, like a magnet.

Often, people looking at their timeline, or experiencing a glimpse of their Divine Contract, feel they 'missed' opportunities or made 'mistakes'. But, as James Joyce said, 'mistakes are the portals of discovery'. Most people have forgotten their divine purpose, partly because, as small children, we are socialised by family and teachers into thinking we have to fit in with the existing social norms. After all, have you ever heard a teacher asking a small child, 'Why are you here? What is your purpose in life?' But many successful people report that they were conscious of what they wanted to do with their lives when they were very young. Our purpose is built in to our very being and we can all discover our own genius if we put our attention on stepping into our remarkable future.

Choosing to fulfil your highest possibility

I have a book in my office. It's only a small book, but it has a very dramatic cover, and its title, in big bold lettering, is: *It's Not How Good You Are, It's How Good You Want To Be*. (The author is Paul Arden and everyone should have a copy! See Recommended books, p. 223.)

When we remember the lives of famous artists, dancers, composers and scientists, we use the word 'genius'. We tend to imagine they were always very good, naturally talented and designed in the womb to be great. But when we look closely and read their own accounts we realise that, not only did they have a natural inclination for their subject, but they had tenacity of purpose. They made choices – often ones that other people thought were completely mad or 'unsuitable' – and they used all their will to become the best in their chosen field. And the 'best' was not just measuring up to what had gone before in their profession, but *excelling*. Often, their immense capacity was not recognised when they were young.

Bob Dylan charmed his family by singing 'Accentuate the positive, eliminate the negative …' when he was only four years old. However his attempt to charm a school audience as a teenager by playing the piano Little Richard style was a disaster! He left university, having never attended classes, set off with hardly any money for New York and hung around the folk scene. Early reports said he was nothing special. But Bob Dylan *wanted* to be special! So he worked at it. He didn't care if he had to scrounge a place to sleep and earned hardly any money when people passed the hat round. This was the destiny he had chosen and he was totally focused.

As we saw earlier, Winston Churchill once told his classmates that one day he would save Britain. How did he know? Was that 'fate' fixed? I think he knew he had the capacity to do something great and, even though he didn't reach his peak until he was in his sixties, the intensity of his desire fuelled his dedication.

Checking your Soul's 'map' and resetting your compass

If your life is a journey, then you need a map of some kind in order to get the most satisfaction from the energy you are putting in to your travels. If you don't make choices about direction or about the kind of landscape you would prefer, you may be condemned to riding in a third-class carriage through grey and featureless lands.

I hope your timeline and your Divine Contract (see p. 35) will have given you a glimpse of the possibilities that you could explore – and, if you feel confused, thinking there is more than one package tour on the menu, just choose something and dedicate yourself to it. Don't look for signs that seem exciting or glamorous. An opportunity or an idea that seems rather insignificant can turn out to be that very special lead that will take you towards a beautiful destiny. And don't be afraid to back down from an activity if you realise it isn't quite right for you. You can change at the next stop. You can reset your compass when you realise you are travelling – not the 'wrong' way, but in a direction that doesn't really convince you that the scenery will be great. It all comes back to choice. You are the captain of your own ship.

10

Brambles On Your Path

When your mind is truly peaceful,
When your heart is full of Love,
Then you will hear the Angels' voices
Singing in the skies above.

THEOLYN CORTENS

What gets in the way?

Everyone knows the fairy tale about Sleeping Beauty, in which the
princess is cursed by the wicked fairy Carabosse and doomed to fall
asleep when she is sixteen years old. When the princess pricks her
finger on a spindle she, the king and queen and the whole court all
fall asleep together and a hedge of brambles and thorns grow up
around the castle. Many princes attempt to cut their way through
the hedge, hoping to wake the princess and make her their bride.
But a hundred years have to pass before the right prince arrives, and
even then he needs magical help from the Lilac Fairy, whose magic
allows the hedge to fall easily away so that the prince can find the
princess and wake her with a kiss.

We can think of our Soul as the princess sleeping in the castle, because we have not managed to carve our way through and declare our love for it. We can also imagine the brambles as our habitual negative thoughts and worries that get in the way of us receiving a helping hand from the Lilac Fairy, who is like our own Guardian Angel.

I want you to consider what unhelpful thoughts, habitual ways of reacting to events and people, or old stories could be contributing to your own hedge of brambles. Then you can go straight into the visualisation below, so that your Guardian Angel can help you to clear the tangle of thorns from your inner garden.

Exercise: Clearing the Brambles in Your Spiritual Path

Start with some questions that might help you identify your thorny issues. Write your answers in your Journal and, using a scale of one to ten, identify whether each one is a really big bramble with deep roots, or just a baby shoot that could easily be nipped in the bud (1 = something that has just started to grow; 10 = a self-replicating monster – when you cut off one twining branch, another two attack you from behind!). Here are some examples:

❖ Do you ever have a sinking feeling when you need to phone a particular person?

❖ Do you feel unable to say what you feel when you experience problems at home or work?

❖ Do you have memories of being bullied or put down when you were young?

❖ Do you have a sense that something invisible prevents you from expressing your real desires? Perhaps as though you have a hidden treasure that cannot shine in the light of day? Maybe you are frightened that someone will criticise, mock or attack you in some way?

❖ Do you recognise that negative responses, such as envy, resent-ment, powerlessness or anger arise when you think about your life? Do any particular topics bring those feelings up – money issues, relationships, or frustrations in your working life?

❖ Make a list of any people in your life, from childhood to the pres-ent day, who provoke any of these negative responses.

❖ Identify your biggest, most difficult 'bramble' and make a com-mitment to clear it with the help of your Guardian Angel. Say aloud: 'I am in charge of my own inner castle and I can clear any negativ-ity that prevents me from experiencing the unconditional Love of the Divine. I am on a journey to meet my Soul and the brambles that get in my way are melting as I surrender myself to Divine Love.'

Now move on to the visualisation exercise:

Visualisation: Clearing the Brambles from Your Spiritual Path

❖ You are sitting on the sofa again, in the beautiful sitting room, looking out into the garden (see p. 67). But on this occasion, your mind feels unsettled, as though you have forgotten something.

❖ You get up from the sofa and turn away from the garden towards a door at the back of the room. As you go through the door, you see a short staircase that is a bit grubby, with quite a few cobwebs hanging around. You are not frightened, but you don't feel very happy. Somehow, you know you need to do a bit of clearing in this part of your house, so you bravely go down a few more steps until you find a rusty old door at the bottom.

❖ With a bit of a push, you manage to open the door and you find yourself outside, in a rambling kitchen garden. There are old plant pots and a few rusty garden tools lying around. You can see a brick pathway ahead of you, but it is covered with stinging nettles and brambles.

❖ This doesn't look pretty at all! You wish that you were back in that beautiful garden, on your way to your sacred space where you would be able to meet your Guardian Angel.

❖ Then, quite suddenly, you feel that magical presence around you once again and you realise that, wherever you are, whatever the problems that surround you, your Guardian Angel is a constant source of help and wisdom.

❖ Your Guardian seems to be whispering to you: 'Let's get started … it won't be as hard as it looks.'

❖ You put a firm foot on the path and take a good look at the first bramble that's in your way. Imagine that bramble has a face, a bit like one of those cross little gargoyles you see on a church. It might even be a face you recognise!

❖ Now take some time for a conversation with this bramble, asking it to tell you why it is blocking your way. Ask what it represents. Often brambles are fears, so you may have to uncover what fears are getting in your way.

(Short silence.)

❖ When you have got an idea what this tangle of brambles might represent, you then need to use your magic eradication technique. Look at your hands and see them shining with light. Stretch out a hand towards the bramble and seize it firmly. Lift it out of the ground and bring its mean little face right up close to your own and say: 'I am a divine being and you have no power over me.'

❖ Now watch as the light from your hand fills the bramble with light and it transforms into a beautiful rose.

❖ You look ahead and see that the brick pathway is clear for you to walk along. As you walk with the rose in your hand, other beautiful flowers, jasmine, lilies, lilacs spring up beside you, filling the air with their beautiful scent.

❖ You realise that the brick pathway has taken you around in a big circle and you see the gate to your garden in front of you.

❖ As you stand at the gate, you realise that you can choose – you can turn down along the country path and go back to the wood to find your sacred space, or you can go back into your sitting room. And there are two pathways to the sitting room: one is through the garden and back through the French windows; the other is back along the brick path through the kitchen garden. Somehow you know that the cobwebs on that old staircase will have all been dusted away before you arrive. The brambles have been cleared from your path and there are no blocks in your way, whichever route you take.

(Short silence.)

❖ After taking your chosen path back to your sitting room, you find yourself once more back in your chair in the everyday world and feel your body resting on the seat.

My students always have a lot of fun with the bramble visualisation. On several occasions, I have had reports that the brambles pop up, not with someone else's face on, but with a mirror image of the person who is doing their inner gardening! One very experienced meditator saw two brambles, each with her own face on, one of which was trying to strangle the other. We discussed whether this might mean an internal struggle, because she was not articulating something that wanted to find expression; so one bramble was trying to silence the other in order to get a chance to be heard.

Interpreting visual images that come up during visualisations is rather like interpreting dreams. If something crops up that you find difficult to understand, it can be very useful to talk to a trusted friend. Another person may be able to get a handle on the essence of your image, because they can see a perspective that is a blind spot for you.

Other comments confirmed that people invariably recognise that the brambles represent negative emotions, such as jealousy and fear. For instance, one student realised she had fallen into the trap of finding other people responsible and then saw the image of a rose during her daily meditation. This prompted lots of discussions about compost and how people try to rebalance alkaline and acid soils. Perhaps that is what we are doing when we look at our Soul's growth – looking at the nutrients that we need and replacing soil that does not support us.

Wrestling with gremlins

When you are small, events and people in your life can provoke big responses in your psyche that can stay with you, even if in later life you can't remember the feelings you had at the time. The response can be like a repeating message on a telephone and can become encoded in your behaviour patterns, until you are hardly aware that it is ruling your life. Visualisations can help us dive deep into our unconscious, enabling us to scout around for gremlins and face them out, so they get their comeuppance. (The word 'gremlin' was used by British pilots in the Second World War when they experi-enced unexplained sabotage to their planes – almost as though they thought a supernatural entity was at work.) But it's important to remember that anything in your life that feels like a 'negative entity' or a 'curse' is really some activity in your psyche that has developed its own agenda and is creating outer manifestations without your conscious permission.

Each one of us has the power to manifest a life of harmony, abundance and beauty. But if that seems to be constantly out of your reach, it may be because 'brambles' or 'gremlins' (whatever you want to call them) have occupied a corner of your psyche and you are letting them run the show. Your Soul should be the monarch in your kingdom. Is your palace being run by unruly servants? If so, you need to challenge them and take back your power. Your Guardian Angel can help you to negotiate a new deal, hiring and firing where necessary.

Dreamtime

The process of uncovering old blocks, anxieties and fears that are stuck in your subconscious can sometimes seem like an ongoing excavation at an archaeological dig. But if there does seem to be something going on that keeps cropping up, creating negative patterns in your life, then it is really worth the digging. By working with your Guardian Angel, you are on a quest that can lead to remarkable revelations. These may come to you during meditation, or you may have helpful dreams, so do keep a notebook by your bed and record any dreams that seem significant, even if the content is mysterious and you don't understand it at first. (When dreams are based on old fears and anxieties they can be pretty scary.)

Being a teacher and offering my services to people who want to solve their difficult issues by working with spiritual guides and Angels, gives me the opportunity to root out some of my own brambles. While I was teaching the first 'Your Guardian Angel Needs You!' eClass, I had a particular dream that helped me clear a very old blockage:

THE OLD HOUSE DREAM

For many years, I had dreams in which old buildings were part of the main theme. In these dreams something was hidden, or I was hiding something myself, not wanting people to know about it. Sometimes, these were real nightmares and I knew something in my psyche needed clearing, but I couldn't seem to resolve it. Perhaps there was a deep-seated anxiety that might explain why I frequently moved house, often with negative results. There was a restless quality underpinning my life and I was sure that if I could pin down the source of the anxiety it would make a big difference.

In the spring of 2010 I was teaching in Gloucestershire and I had booked accommodation for the trip on the internet. The taxi driver who picked me up at the station was surprised when I gave him the address. 'That's not a hotel,' he said. 'That's a pub.' He knew the place well and said he didn't know they offered bed and breakfast.

It was dark when he dropped me off at the pub. It was a large building several stories high, on a main road in Gloucester and well lit from the outside. It was a Friday night and I could see people coming and going in the bar downstairs, but when I looked up I could see what seemed to be empty windows without curtains. I felt a bit uncertain. The house looked rather unloved. What had I let myself in for? The landlady took me upstairs and along corridors, all carpeted, but a bit shabby. It certainly wasn't five-star accommodation, but everything was clean and tidy, and I slept quite peacefully while I was there for two nights.

After I returned home, I had another dream about an old house, but I realised that it had been triggered by the visit to the pub. I dreamed I was in a large, bare room, dancing lightly and joyfully like a fairy, when I noticed a man in blue overalls taking up some floorboards in the corner. He was tinkering with wires under the boards. I was suspicious, but he showed me his official plastic badge that confirmed he was a genuine telephone repairman. I felt nervous and ran down some stairs, where I bumped into more men wearing workmen's clothes. The house was large, uncarpeted and neglected. I decided to go back up the stairs and noticed there were piles of old clothes scattered around. But then someone came up behind me and I was terrified. I screamed and woke myself up!

It took me a few days to sort out the layers of meaning in the dream:

As a toddler, I had lived in a large house in west London where my mother was housekeeper. There was a walled garden with flowers and a pleasant sitting room with books – a very charming, middle-class home. I was four years old when my mother remarried and I was taken to live in the country. Our flat was at the top of an old mill, had no running water, no carpets and very little furniture. My stepfather was in love with my mother and did his best to be a good father, but we were uncomfortable in this new relationship. I found it difficult to share my mum, who I had had to myself for several years; he found it difficult to enjoy the role of being father to someone else's child. Small children easily pick up on hidden resentments, which can be nearly as dangerous as open hostility. I was probably missing the lovely couple from the London house, who had no children of their own and used to make quite a fuss of me. My stepfather worked for the Post Office as a telecommunications engineer and my mother told me that when he came back from work he would get very angry if my toys were scattered on the stairs. I think I must have felt very insecure.

You can see the ingredients for the dream piecing themselves together here! As a little girl, my sense of joy and fun
had been threatened by the negative responses of my stepfather, represented in my dream by the man tinkering with the
wiring, as well as the one coming up behind me on the stairs,
who frightened me. I remembered that I used to be scared at
night and was told to go back to bed. As a child, I felt I could-
n't ask my mother for her support during the night, so I
realised that the telephone man in my dream represented a
disconnection of lines of communication. The dream was
showing me the source of two significant patterns in my life:
the first was the sense of discomfort at home, leading to a restless need to move house; the second was a reluctance to
communicate my needs, since I had kept them to myself from
a young age, assuming that no one would be there to support
me.

My dream is an example of the way your psyche will reveal its
hidden secrets if you persist. But, most importantly, in a dream you
can have a direct experience of how a situation felt at the time,
whether it was something quite small or very serious. What might
seem like a minor event, such as someone being cross because your
toys were left out, may easily have made a very big impression on
you as a small child. It is the sensation of fear and anxiety, which has
been stuck in our psyche for years, that we can re-experience in a
dream. It wasn't as though I did not already 'know' things that might
have affected me – I had some conscious memories of the flat in the
mill and my mother had described our life there. Also, the scary stuff
wasn't to do with any one dramatically unpleasant event. But the
dream put me directly in touch with the feelings I had experienced
as a four-year-old.

By realising the effects that old responses can have, you can reach insights that put a new perspective on how you do things, as well as how you respond to people and events in the present day. A revelation of this kind can lead to huge changes in your outer life.

Small steps lead to giant strides towards your destination

The exercises and the visualisations in this book have been designed as an unfolding process. First, we ask questions about our life, identifying the story of how we got here, right now, doing whatever it is we are doing. Next, we look for signs that will help to give us an overview of why we came here in the first place – we want to identify our underlying purpose. Then we set about clearing anything that is holding us in an unhelpful place. Whether we see these as old brambles and bindweed in a garden, or as gremlins getting in our way, what we are trying to do is to return to a reasonably 'clean slate'. In the next stage of our journey we will start opening our inner shutters to allow more light into our lives. Remember, your Guardian Angel is with you, calling you – you need to come together!

11

Karmic Spring Cleaning

Your Guardian Angel and karmic releasing

Karma is a Sanskrit word that is difficult to explain, but loosely translated, it means 'cause and effect'. In other words, according to karmic law, anything that is done will naturally provoke a sequence of events. Whether we call these events 'good' or 'bad' is very subjective. A 'bad' event can sometimes bring us up sharp and cause us to change our behaviour for the better. Someone could win a great deal of money and would certainly think, at the time, that this was 'good'. But the sudden wealth might set the winner on a path of chaotic living, with no regard to their own health or the feelings of others. As I was writing this chapter, my husband Will pointed out a newspaper story about a man who won nine million pounds and became seriously depressed. The winner said he'd never thought a dream of his could possibly come true and now he felt he couldn't have any more dreams, because he could make them come true immediately, with the power of his purse. The man said that whenever he saw someone in the newspaper shop buying a lottery ticket, he always advised them against spending their money, just in case they would win and become as miserable as he. The man died only five years after winning and his friends said the prize had ruined him. One person's blessing is another person's poison.

If, when we look at our timeline, we can see that our behaviour has at any stage triggered a series of events that we feel were 'bad', we can easily get caught up in a guilt trip. However, the more we feel guilty, the more we are imprisoned by the karmic process. Freedom from the cycle of karma happens when we disentangle our emotions from the story and see it from a new perspective. Our personal histories have happened over a period of time that can be charted using human measurements: days, weeks, months and years. For the most part, we know what has happened, and when – there are photographs, certificates, diaries and memories that will verify our biographies. Even if you ceremoniously burn all physical records of a past that was upsetting, your history doesn't go away. However, any meaning the story has for us, any hold it has over our emotional and spiritual life, is entirely subjective.

When you review your history, you need to become alert to the hidden messages, the repeating patterns and themes that we all tend to overlook because we are living our lives from day to day, just dealing with what comes up as best we can. Only when you stand back and see your past as a story, one that you have been writing with 'me' as the main character, do you get an opportunity to engage with the powerful possibility that you could create a new twist for the plot. Your Guardian Angel, as Navigator for your Soul's 'ship of life', can help you find an overview of your journey so far and will help to lift any burdens or guilt that are weighing you down. Think of your ship, not as a galleon on the sea, but as an air balloon. It is time to dump some ballast over the side, so that your balloon can rise higher into the skies.

The following visualisation is designed to help you regain a sense of inner strength and power. When you look at your life as a story, or as if it was a movie, and realise that *you* are the author, *you* are the movie director, then you will feel completely in charge of the way your own life unfolds. *You* are the person who decides on the beginning, the middle and the end of the story of your life. Why not make it a winner? The power is in your hands and your Guardian Angel will always be there for you, even if you have to rewrite a chapter or shoot a new 'take'. You don't need to make a movie like anyone else's; use all the Technicolor that life offers – be brave, be bold, be amazing!

As this visualisation may bring up a few tears, make sure you are prepared with some paper tissues. Although I am sure it will also have the potential to make you laugh.

Visualisation: Healing the Past

❖ Find yourself once again in your lovely sitting room (see p. 67), gazing out of the window, watching the flowers and the trees bending gently in the summer breeze.

❖ From your sofa, you can enjoy the beauty of the garden, but there is some sadness in the back of your mind.

❖ Get up from the sofa and walk through the French windows into your garden once again. Notice your sad feelings as you wander through the gate and along the country lane.

❖ As you walk, you are thinking about the cause of your sadness. What can it be? Is it to do with an old relationship with a parent, a child, a lover?

❖ Unravel your memory of the story that is troubling you. How long has this sadness been with you?

❖ You are walking along the path in the woods towards your sacred building, but your heart is heavy with these old memories. Do not try to keep the memories and the old feelings at bay. Allow your-self to cry, if that is how you feel.

❖ When you arrive at the door of your sacred space, you can let all your feelings come up. You feel yourself surrounded by the loving presence of your Guardian Angel, who encourages you to sit on your special seat.

❖ Through your tears you can see in front of you a large screen and there seems to be a black and white movie being shown on it. Your crying calms down as you pay attention to the story being acted out on the screen.

❖ After a while, you realise that the story is the very same set of events that you were just remembering – the ones that had made you so unhappy. You can see the people involved, including yourself, as characters in the movie. Your Guardian Angel's loving presence seems to be saying: 'There you are, it's just a story. It's just an old movie after all. You can watch it as many times as you like. Here is the box with the replay button. You just stay here, watching it over and over again.'

❖ The idea of seeing this movie played over and over again seems really boring. You get a bit restless in your seat. 'Yes,' whispers your Guardian's voice in your ear, 'It is really boring isn't it? Wouldn't it be dreadful to have to watch this film over and over again, for ever and ever?'

❖ You are very pleased to discover that you might have a way out. Your Guardian Angel explains: 'The box has a stop button on it as well. You can choose: replay or stop. Which is to be?'

❖ You hesitate. Part of you cannot let go of your story. After all, it has been with you for a long time and has some people from your past in it. Some of them, you realise, were not bad people – there were just some misunderstandings.

❖ Your Guardian Angel asks: 'Do you want to say goodbye to some people in your story?'

❖ That seems like a good idea and, as you watch, the characters in the black-and-white movie step down into your room in full colour as flesh-and-blood people. You stand up to meet them, one by one. This is your chance to speak to them; to offer them your love and blessings.

❖ Take your time now to talk to anyone who is part of your old story. Share your old sadness. Let them know that you have grown up; that you are wiser and would like to heal the past.

❖ Now you have finished sharing your old story and made everything feel better between you. There are lots of hugs and tears, but every-one is happy to say goodbye for the last time. The characters from your story return to the screen and you see them back in the black-and-white movie, waving to you as the credits roll, saying:

THE END

❖ You sit there, clapping as the movie screen goes blank and the cur-tains close. You feel full of joy and you can feel your Guardian Angel wrapping you up in a cosy blanket of love. 'So that's all right now, isn't it?' comes a whisper in your ear. You nod in agreement. It feels much, much better. As though a great load has been lifted from your mind.

❖ Your Guardian Angel guides you to the door that opens gently, so that you can step back on to the shining path. Your heart is as light as a feather and you find yourself running and skipping happily back through the wood, along the country lane and through the garden until you reach the French windows that lead to the sitting room.

❖ Now you find yourself back on your chair in the everyday world.

Susie's story is a very powerful example of the way our own inner work can provoke responses from our immediate circle of family or friends. Even if people around us are unaware of the spiritual development we have committed to, when we change our own inner vibrations, there will often be noticeable responses from them. Sometimes quite surprising events will take place.

SUSIE'S EXPERIENCE

I had recently been trying to put closure on some past issues, so the visualisation came at a good time for me. As I watched, the cinema curtains opened and my life story began. As the black-and-white movie played, I got the tissue box out and had a good old sob, but once the credits rolled I felt a sense of relief. I had the best night's sleep in a long while and in the morning I felt so much lighter. Even though a few memories crept back in, some of them actually made me smile and, because they were all in black and white, that made a huge difference. I could see the memories for what they were – out-of-date stories.

A few days later, my mum told me a family secret I had heard of in whispers as a child. It concerned my grandfather who was my childhood hero, because my dad died when I was twelve. When I was small, I had thought that this negative story actually concerned a neighbour, so I was very surprised to hear that my own grandfather had been the 'baddie'. Usually, this kind of revelation would have upset me deeply, but this time I felt no attachment to the story, because (after a deep breath) I managed to put it into 'black and white'. I felt that what I was doing in the Guardian Angel course had created an invisible effect on my mum, which prompted her to share this old story. Maybe she is also beginning to understand that the secrets are better shared and banished into old movies and newspapers, which are only fit for fish and chips!

Another student in my eClass, Mandy, recognised that the repeating scenes in her movie always confirmed her as the victim. She also acknowledged that this ongoing, neverending saga was quite boring.

MANDY'S EXPERIENCE

Some of the scenes in my movie were painful to relive, yet some of them were really joyful. What amazed me was to find some of the storylines being repeated over and over again with new characters, usually with myself cast in a 'poor-me' role. When the movie ended, I thought: How could I have produced something so boring? But I was also able to let go of the resentment I had regarding my upbringing, and found that I could thank my parents for all they have done for me, to the best of their ability. I asked my Guardian Angel to help me get out of the 'poor-me' role, and then I realised I could write myself a new movie – something much more exciting! I also understood that I am a child of the Divine and don't need to feel I am a failure. The idea that the movie does not have to be constantly replayed and that I could press a 'stop' button whenever I liked, made me feel positive and inspired.

Selena had great fun with some of her images. Her version of the exercise was to picture her life in static pictures, using the image of an album of old photos.

SELENA'S EXPERIENCE

I found it easier to think of my life as black-and-white pictures in a photo album. Pictures from my childhood, teenage years and college days flooded back into my mind. Many happy times were recorded in my album, but also the recent, more painful times, which I was trying to shut down. But now there was no pain and I was able to look at all the pictures, acknowledging both the good times and the bad. I did have a good cry. Then I tried rewriting the script and pictures. I knew what I wanted and my present reality wasn't anything like my dream. I felt there was a gap that could not be closed. So I said goodbye to my Guardian Angel and shut my album.

A short while later, I thought I would try again. This time, in addition to the characters that appear in my history, and myself, I saw my Guardian Angel popping up in all the pictures. I noticed my responses to my Guardian Angel's presence and the promptings in each picture. Suddenly, all the characters faded and I started 'seeing' what my Guardian had been trying to tell me. It was like being taught how to write in primary school, learning to cross the 't' and dot the 'i', or to use a capital letter or full stop. In every life situation, my Guardian had answered my questions when I was perplexed. Why *should* I put a dot on the 'i'? In other words, why should I behave a certain way in my situation, when other people don't? My Guardian would just say, 'Go on try it'. As I looked at the pictures showing the times I had listened to my Guardian's advice and acted accordingly, I could see what amazing results there had been!

I turned the pages in this album of me and my Guardian Angel. I saw a progression of pictures of myself with all kinds of facial expressions: exasperated, pulling my hair out, yelling and screeching at my Guardian when I couldn't understand the reasons behind my lessons. Slowly, I started smiling and chuckling at myself in those pictures, not always getting the message. Suddenly, a lot of things made sense. Instead of 'Karmic Clearing', I nicknamed my album 'Karmic Laughter' ... and have a smile on my face every time I think about it.

Shedding old stories that limit your progress

The karmic process is perfect and precise. It is also far reaching. In the words of Francis Thompson:

Thou canst not stir a flower
Without troubling of a star

Nothing occurs without a reason and everything that happens follows a series of natural laws that encourage balance and harmony. These laws are very finely tuned, like a complex machine, and we are living in it so, for the most part, we are not aware of the cogs turning. None the less, at a metaphysical level, everything is unfolding as it should. This does not mean that everything is predestined: we are participating in a grand design, but there is no external designer. What is being created is evolving and can be moulded by our thoughts. However, it is not necessarily a simple task to identify the unconscious thoughts that are the foundation of our life as we experience it. And some of our unhelpful thought patterns may well be embedded in us because of parental or social beliefs.

The developers of psychological theories in the nineteenth century, such as Sigmund Freud, identified that there is an unconscious element to our minds, which can create illness and other negative by-products. But modern psychology tends to assume that the content of our unconscious has been harvested during this present life and pays no attention to the possibility that we have lived before, or that we inherit family issues, even if we have never met the family of our biological origin. The ongoing law of karma tells us:

❖ We do not consciously choose when and where we were born, but our Soul will have chosen circumstances that give us an opportunity to evolve. Some circumstances will be challenging, others will be supportive, but we need to accept the hand of cards we have chosen and use it wisely.

❖ Our present life is only one life that we can experience and we may well have lived others, both as a human being or as other kinds of beings, possibly on other planets. And we will probably have many future lives as well.

❖ 'Bad' karma can be reversed through spiritual grace, which is available to everyone who chooses to review their life and adjust their responses and behaviour. There is no 'sin' so wicked that a person cannot find redemption when they open their heart to love.

❖ Choice is always available, however difficult things seem. A victim of negative behaviour has the opportunity to become a saviour. For instance, if someone grows up in a rough neighbourhood, they can go through life feeling hard done by and use this story as an excuse for anti-social behaviour. Or, instead of being a victim of their story, this person could grow up to become a campaigner, with a determination to help improve life for others in the same situation.

By reviewing our present-day life as though it was a movie, we can gain a perspective that allows us to make a choice. We can create an 'Hour of Power', in which we affirm our divine capacity to create a life based on our spiritual wisdom, not on emotional reactions.

Exercise: Hour of Power

Shortly after your movie visualisation, give yourself at least one hour to do the following exercise. For the last part, you will need a mirror to look into. This could be a small hand mirror, but a long mirror would be better – so that you can stand in front of it and see your whole body.

You are going to face some old demons that might seem scary, but demons are containers of energy and you want to be able to use that energy creatively. It is precisely those buried feelings that you have hidden away because you think they are bad that need to be mined for the power they have been consuming – power that you could be using to build a remarkable future. Many famous people describe how anger drove them to take up their power: Bob Geldof was enraged by the plight of the starving Ethiopians and he put on huge rock concerts to raise money for them; Gandhi was furious when he was thrown off a train in South Africa because he was the 'wrong colour' and this experience signalled the beginning of his mission against racial injustice. The very emotions that we fear and attempt to hide can be fuel for creative action. As Jesus said, 'The stone that was rejected becomes the cornerstone' (*Matthew* 21: 42).

❖ Gather together some coloured pencils or pens and a notebook without any lines.

❖ Ask your Guardian Angel to support you in getting in touch with your most difficult feelings.

❖ Quickly write down all the issues in your present life that are creating problems, whether this is in relationships, career, finances, health and so on. Just write down how you feel, allowing yourself to write really nasty comments – no one else will read this! Don't be afraid to get in touch with any seriously negative emotions, the kind you would not like to admit to, like hate, rage, jealousy or anger. Writing quickly will allow suppressed feelings to come to the surface.

You may notice that this process makes you feel a bit shaky, but this is a sign that you have been using a great deal of energy to keep a lid on your less comfortable feelings. The refusal to admit to negative feelings calls for great reserves of creative energy and this stored energy has a magical potency that can be used to recreate your present situation. The reason we are so frightened of getting in touch with these 'dark' responses is that part of us knows how powerful they can be. However, if we don't summon up this power and use it to build our chosen destiny, then it will secretly sabotage us! So, in this 'Hour of Power' you must admit to *all* the hidden resentments and anger that are consuming your creative energies.

In stories about dragons, the beast is always sitting on a pile of treasure. Your 'dragon' is your accumulation of negative thoughts, probably collected over many years; under your dragon are the 'jewels' that you can access, as soon as you persuade the dragon to move out of your way. You don't have to do any slaughtering – you just need to realise that *you* are in charge of the power, not the dragon.

Even before you have finished writing, you will feel a surge of energy, created by your admission that you have been storing hate, jealousy, anger and all those other 'Deadly Sins'. You are reclaiming your gold reserves and can now step into a new scenario.

❖ On a separate piece of paper write the words:

I AM THE CREATIVE POWER IN MY OWN LIFE.

I AM THE CAUSE OF ALL THE EFFECTS I EXPERIENCE AND I CHOOSE TO REDESIGN MY LIFE.

❖ Underneath, write down what you want for yourself and identify how soon you want the change, the event or the required item to arrive. Preface each statement of intent with the words: 'Right now, I am ready to …' (for example, … meet a loving partner; find a new, better-paid job; drive a better car).

❖ Remember how angry you were just now, realising you didn't have these things? Can you still feel all that energy stirring in you?

❖ Look into your mirror, either a small one so that you can look into your own face. Or stand in front of a long mirror. Either way, gaze into your own eyes as you read out the statements that affirm your creative power, followed by each separate 'Right now, I am ready …' intention. Declaim everything as loudly as you can and, with each intention, make a physical gesture that feels strong; you could stamp your foot, you could push your fist into the air, whatever makes you feel powerful.

❖ Now destroy your 'hate and rage' pages, but keep your creative intentions. Put the date on the bottom.

❖ Wait *impatiently* for the results!

Taking up your own power, so that you measure your results on your own terms, not on ideas supplied by your family 'tribe', or by your society, can be a tough challenge. You may start to notice some people around you reacting when they experience the new energy that will radiate around you. They may or may not like the new you, but now is the time to develop the real you. No more hiding your light under a bushel!

12

Taking Down the Shutters

*For if you should see a man shut up in a closed
room ... and you wished to make him truly happy,
you would begin by blowing out all his lamps; and
then throw open the shutters to let in the light of
Heaven.*

SAMUEL RUTHERFORD

Your Guardian Angel helps you to increase your spiritual awareness

The process of dismantling the old knots and tangles in our psyche, accumulated over many years, possibly over many lifetimes, allows the light of our pure consciousness to start shining through. Your Guardian Angel is cheering you on all the way, because this is an essential part of spiritual development. How can we let our light spread? How can we shine in the world if our psychic windows are all grimy? And how can we see into the world if our shutters are up? Another image we might use for our state of consciousness is that of a pool of water. When we look into our pool, is it crystal clear to the bottom? Or are there clumps of weed, dead fish and old rubbish, ancient leather boots and rusty tin cans cluttering the view, preventing the water from shining like silver?

Your Guardian Angel cannot drag your pond for you – this work is yours. But your Guardian will be there, encouraging, consoling and protecting you when the going seems tough. You might think, as I have often done myself: How many times have I struggled with that old bit of junk that I want to get rid of? At first you thought it was just an old cola can, but sometimes it seems immovable, like a huge fridge that was dumped deep in your pool and has become silted up with mud. Sometimes shifting these old blocks needs great commitment and persistence and you certainly need plenty of spiritual and moral support from your Guardian Angel and personal friends on the same journey.

Expanding your consciousness to include all Creation in your compassion

As your mystical awareness grows, you will find that the view from your spiritual windows expands. It will expand inwardly, so that you are able to easily access different dimensions and experience messages from your Guardian Angel, Archangels and other non-physical helpers. It will expand outwardly, and you will feel the love in your heart extending to embrace the world around you, so that your compassion becomes more and more inclusive. Not only will you experience love for the beauty of Creation and all its variety, but you will find it easier to love your fellow human beings – even those you might have thought were not at all lovable.

Much of the time our experience of ourselves is narrow, like a camera with a small aperture, because we have to focus on very necessary everyday matters. Then, sometimes, we have a breakthrough, perhaps triggered by a special occasion, like a quiet moment in a leafy glade, or on a mountaintop, or at the birth of a baby. Then our camera lens opens up and the vista becomes enlarged. We notice our sense of being growing larger and feel that we can love everything we see. An effective meditation practice allows our camera lens to open gradually to a wider aperture, so that we see our world through expanded consciousness more regularly. Over time, we gain a sense of always being pure spirit while at the same time working and functioning in the material world.

Your commitment adds to the spiritual development of all humanity

In the mid-1970s many people started to talk about the 'Hundredth Monkey' effect. This idea developed after biologists observing macaque monkeys on the Japanese island of Koshima in 1952 noticed some of their number washing their sweet potatoes before eating them. This new behaviour spread to younger monkeys in the usual fashion, by observation and repetition. Once the number of monkeys adopting this habit had passed one hundred, monkeys on other islands started to wash their sweet potatoes as well – even though they had never been in contact with the first group. Other creatures provide similar examples. Between the two World Wars, dairy companies in Britain invented cardboard lids for their milk bottles, but small birds, especially bluetits and robins, who were used to being able to steal milk from the top of unprotected bottles, soon found the cardboard lids easy to open. Then came the aluminium foil lids and the birds had a new problem to deal with. The bluetits very quickly learnt to pierce the new milk tops, and by the mid-1970s bird watchers realised that the entire British population of around one million bluetits had learned how to open the foil lids. The trick had rapidly spread among the whole species. Strangely the robins never did get turned on to the same habit!

In 1954, scientists from the University of Melbourne, Australia, published remarkable results after teaching rats how to navigate a hazardous maze to reach food. They discovered that other rats would very quickly be able to make their way safely through the maze, even though they had not learned the behaviour directly from the first group. The scientists concluded that there was a group rat consciousness, which allowed the invisible transmission of information. Rupert Sheldrake (see Recommended books, p. 223) believes this kind of consciousness will be found in all species. He calls this group awareness 'morphic resonance' and says it explains telepathy and intuition.

These examples demonstrate that the consciousness of a species is shared, even if the individuals are not physically close to each other. It is the same for humanity: if a small group meditates, the effect will ripple throughout the human population. We may not see dramatic results immediately, but we will begin to notice small shifts. When we set up meditation groups in our community it is possible to measure positive results, such as a fall in stress levels leading to fewer road accidents and crimes.

So, everything we are doing for ourselves on this journey with our Guardian Angel has a powerful effect on the human race and, since we are the most powerful creatures on the planet, this will have a positive effect on planet Earth as well.

The next magical visualisation takes you through the 'Gates of Light', which are portals to the inner dimensions that give you access to higher states of consciousness. It is long and takes you into very deep realms, so please allow yourself enough time for preparation and grounding. Don't try to squeeze it into an evening, but use some of your time out, such as a weekend or holiday.

Visualisation: Journey Through the Gates of Light

❖ As you breathe deeply and gently, allow your mind to wander back to your favourite sofa (see p. 67). Once more, you are looking out through the French windows into the beautiful garden.

❖ You get up from the sofa and wander through the garden until you find the gate that leads out into the country. You walk down the lane, listening to the sounds of Nature, watching the magical colours in the corn fields and occasionally gazing at the clear blue skies above you.

❖ Now you are in the woods again, following the familiar path back to your own special place, your sacred building that is always there, waiting for you, whenever you want to go there.

❖ Once more, the doors open to welcome you and, when you step inside, you experience the loving energy of your Divine friend and companion, your Guardian Angel.

❖ Your Guardian Angel sends you a whispered message: 'Today we are going on a special journey and you will be given a new vision of your possibilities.'

❖ You are led towards the shining staircase that you ascended on a previous journey. You stand on the first step and find yourself moving upwards, through the blue skies, past the clouds that look like feathers, where Angels are singing and playing wonderful music on their lutes. Your Guardian Angel is beside you as a presence and you can feel his or her love is with you.

❖ This time, you go beyond the blue summer skies, up and up through night skies, and you watch as the stars come out, twinkling against the indigo-blue background. Eventually, you arrive at a golden platform with filigree gates and you step through them into a beautiful room that seems to be made of crystal. Even the floor is shining with jewels.

❖ A golden Angel comes towards you and offers you a bunch of golden keys. There are seven keys and the Angel shows you a gate across the other side of the room, indicating that you can open the gate if you choose, using one of the keys.

❖ In your heart and mind you are wondering what will happen – what will be on the other side of the gate?

❖ You will be transformed, comes a thought in your mind. You know the thought has been sent by your Guardian Angel. Are you ready for the first transformation?

❖ You glide across the room and open the gate. Light floods through you and rushes around your whole being. The light is soft, but you feel that it is determined to fill every tiny part of you. It is a magical experience and you enjoy the tingling sensation that washes through all of your cells.

❖ 'Trust the Light,' says the Angel of the Keys. 'This is the first transformation: trust the Light.'

❖ Stay with this light, allowing its soft energy to wrap itself around you, so that you feel supported and comforted.

(Short silence.)

❖ Through the light you can see the shape of another gate. You find another key and open it. More light moves towards you; like a stream of water it wraps itself around you. You can hear music and the sounds of harmonious singing.

❖ 'Listen to the messages from Heaven,' says the Angel of the Keys. 'This is the second transformation: your ears are opened to messages from celestial beings. Are you ready to open the next gate?'

❖ The light is surrounding you and you can still hear the music and the singing.

(Short silence.)

❖ You open the next gate and find yourself washed in warm, pink light that soothes every particle in your body, easing away all the tension you have been carrying.

❖ 'Accept the Love that is freely given,' says the Angel of the Keys. 'This is the third transformation: learning to give and receive Love is the key to understanding all things.'

❖ As you feel the energy of this light filling your whole being, you notice that all your old tensions and anxieties have floated away.

(Short silence.)

❖ 'Now is the time use your fourth key.'

❖ The light from the fourth gate is red like fire and you feel invigorated as it sparkles around you, like leaping flames that want to lift you up. You feel energy pulsing through your veins and through all your cells.

❖ 'Take this light and use it wisely. It is the divine life force in action. Do not allow it to sleep in you, but take it out into the world and let it shine brightly through everything that you do.'

❖ You feel transformed by this light, as though you are reborn with a fresh source of vitality.

(Short silence.)

❖ Ahead of you is the fifth gate, filled with a radiance that glows like the rising sun. Even before you unlock the gate, long rays of glorious light stream out towards you and cloak you in a shining mantle. The Angel speaks once more: 'Divine glory fills the world with its great majesty. Accept this radiance into your life and you will be filled with confidence and courage. Your heart will always be strong and you will radiate sunshine wherever you go.'

❖ As you sit in this light, you can feel a light beginning to glow in your solar plexus and your heart. The light is warm and fills you with new certainty about your life.

(Short silence.)

❖ Now you can see the sixth gate and a new, white light is calling you towards it. You are surprised by the cool sensation that you experience when you step through the gate. There is a snowy crispness in the air and everywhere seems to be bathed in silver. The Angel of the Keys tells you: 'This light is a gift that brings maturity, discipline and focus. Without this challenge, all the other gifts of light you have received cannot be realised. The light seeks a structure in order to manifest from the abstract and the invisible, and this is what you can feel as coolness. Accept the light in all its manifestations and you will be able to express your divine nature and realise your highest potential.'

❖ You sit for a moment, allowing the cool sensation to settle into your whole being. You experience this as a calming process. A new serenity and a sense of grace fill you. You do not lose your connection to the warm light you have experienced at the other gates, but somehow you feel a new power arising in you. The power of choice and the knowledge that you can use Divine Energy effectively.

(Short silence.)

❖ The seventh gate is studded with coloured jewels and the light glows like an amethyst crystal.

❖ As you walk through the gate, this majestic light spreads itself around the floor so that you are walking on a glowing carpet of purple light. You seem to be in a great cathedral of light, with stained-glass windows through which many coloured lights are streaming. You turn around and look backwards through all the open gates towards the place you came from and see a rainbow of colours. Once more, the Angel speaks to you: 'Be prepared to take back your knowledge of the light into your world. Remember the glory and majesty you have experienced: the comfort, the power and the healing, the splendour and the serenity. All these qualities are available for you at all times.'

❖ You look around you for a moment, enjoying the sensations and acknowledging the grandeur of the divine light in all its colours.

(Short silence.)

❖ Now you are being led back through the gates and each one closes behind you in turn.

❖ Eventually, you arrive back at the room with the jewelled floor and your Guardian Angel ushers you to the top of the moving staircase.

❖ Gently and smoothly you are moved downwards: through the night skies and past the stars; down through the summer blue skies, where the Angels are singing; down towards the open roof of your special sacred room.

❖ You find yourself back in your room with your Guardian Angel beside you. The colours of the lights you have experienced are still with you as you walk towards the door that leads to the path that will take you back to your sitting room.

❖ Slowly and calmly, you walk through the wood, along the country lane, through the gate and into the garden. You wander across the green lawn, smelling the flowers, listening to the birds and the insects, touching the bark of trees as you walk. Then you come back into the sitting room and sit on your sofa.

❖ Gradually, you feel yourself back in the everyday world on your chair and start to ground yourself.

Veronique, a Reiki teacher who had already worked with Angels for many years, was given a series of very clear messages and reminders as she travelled with the Angel of the Keys. She sent over this report on our discussion board:

VERONIQUE'S MESSAGES

I noticed that each message had great significance:

❖ In time of fear: 'Trust the light.'
❖ Whenever I am lost as to what to do: 'Listen to the messages from the heavens.'
❖ When I fear being rejected: 'Learn to give and receive Love.'
❖ Whenever I have had a wonderful meditation and I am filled with light: 'Do not allow it to sleep in you, but take it out into the world . . .'
❖ Whenever I fear not being good enough: 'Accept this radiance into your life and you will be filled with confidence and courage. Your heart will always be strong and you will radiate sunshine wherever you are.'
❖ Whenever I lack discipline: 'This light is a gift that brings maturity, discipline and focus. Without this challenge, all other gifts of light you have received cannot be realised.'
❖ And finally, when I am snowed under by problems and challenges: 'Remember the glory and majesty you have experienced – the comfort, the power and the healing, the

splendour and the serenity. All these qualities are available for you at all times.'

Today, after listening to all these messages with great attention, I felt wonderful. I was left filled with enthusiasm and great hope. Life is meant to be lived with joy and in awe.

Teresa did not hear messages or words of wisdom, but experienced different colours and physical sensations that left her feeling blissful.

TERESA'S EXPERIENCE

The visualisation took me to this wonderful golden Angel. I saw her as a huge Angel with massive golden wings. I felt so peaceful and happy that she was waiting there just for me. She showed me the keys and they were made of glowing silver; they seemed so eager to be used. At each gate, I was filled with beautiful colours that were so bright and unlike the ones we see on Earth. The light was flowing through my body and filled every cell. I felt this warm and glowing light fill my heart area.

As I went through each gate I felt something different happening to me right away. Waves of light and colours hit me and embraced me. Finally, I came to the cathedral, where I was overwhelmed by the beauty, the light and the serenity; it was pure bliss. I wanted to stay there and feel my connection with the Divine.

After the visualisation, I was calm and happy and I could feel the warm, embracing wings of my Guardian Angel around me. This was a journey I will never forget. I now want to take these experiences and feelings I had into my everyday life, knowing I can feel this peaceful and centred when I need to.

Every person who experiences these inspiring visions, and begins to understand that we can access wisdom and joy by reconnecting to our Divine Source, will find their life enriched in countless ways. Because we are all connected to each other by threads of light energy rooted in the Source of all being, our individual experiences will add to the whole sum of human experience and will help to shift old, stuck patterns, fears and anxieties that are lodged in humanity's collective psyche.

It is said that the clear spiritual intention of one Swiss holy man, Brother Klaus, kept the Nazis out of Switzerland. Imagine how we can transform the world, if we all turn our hearts and minds to working in harmony with the power that creates and sustains us!

13

Jacob's Ladder

*And he dreamed, and behold a ladder set up on the
earth, and the top of it reached to Heaven: and
behold the angels of God ascending and descending
on it.*

GENESIS 28:12

Mystical maps

Most mystical traditions, from all kinds of different cultures and historical periods, offer us maps and diagrams that help to explain the inner processes we encounter on the road to becoming fully realised human beings. If we want to live up to our full potential, we have to explore the breadth and depth of our own possibilities, and these spiritual maps are an attempt to identify the different stages we are likely to experience.

In the biblical story about the patriarch, Jacob, we read about a ladder that allowed the Angels to come up and down between Heaven and Earth (*Genesis* 28: 11–19). The ladder is a very old spiritual metaphor – it suggests that the process of spiritual development means starting at the bottom rung on a ladder and climbing to the top. The word 'ascension' is associated with this model, but it does also suggest that we leave some 'lower' aspects of ourselves behind. I find 'expansion' a more useful word – we don't lift ourselves up and beyond the world, instead we expand our consciousness to become more inclusive. As we've already seen, we usually experience life through a very small aperture, but we can open it wider to allow more light and wisdom to enter our consciousness.

One very useful idea is the Four Worlds map found in the Jewish mystical tradition of Kabbalah. In ancient cultures philosophers

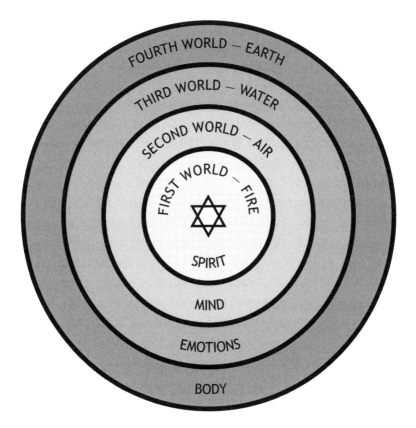

The Four Worlds

believed that everything in Creation derives from four elements – Fire, Air, Water and Earth. The human being has four 'bodies' that correspond to these elements: a spiritual body (Fire); a mental body (Air); an emotional body (Water); and a physical body (Earth). All four of our bodies have to be in balance and integrated in order for us to become whole and complete. Think of a bicycle wheel with some spokes missing or loose, and how this will make the bike wobble. In the same way, if one of our bodies in underdeveloped, we will wobble too. Something will be missing from our lives. If our spiritual, mental, emotional and physical bodies are in harmony with each other, they will work together like the wheels on the most expensive racing bike ever built.

Our Spirit provides the energy to feed Mind and Emotions, after which our physical Body and our material environment are manifested. Our Mind and Emotions play a key role in the outer results. Even if we have powerful spiritual desires, we may not be able to realise them in the world if mental and emotional issues create those brambles we have just been dealing with (see p. 111).

In the centre of the diagram I have put a six-pointed star to represent our Soul, which is connected to the Divine Source. The six-pointed star is made up of two triangles – one pointing to Heaven and one to Earth. Is your Soul still asleep, like the princess whose castle is surrounded by briars and brambles? In many fairy stories and myths, the health of the king or other ruler represents the health of the whole country. Our Soul never sleeps and is always present for us. But if we have forgotten she is there, then how can our mental, emotional and physical bodies be healthy? But if we go on a journey to reconnect with our Soul, we will be able to stand at the centre of our inner castle and look out across the landscape of the Mind, Emotions and physical Body, and nourish it with love. Every time we meditate, we have an opportunity to peep into that inner castle and, over time, the door will open more easily.

Sometimes, the Four Worlds are shown as a chain, creating layers from the 'Crown' of the Tree of Life down to the 'Kingdom' at the bottom.

In this diagram we do see a ladder effect, but the Kabbalists, although they wanted to make a mystical 'ascension' in order to commune with Angels and perhaps get a glimpse of the Divine Throne, placed a great emphasis on 'descending' – bringing Heaven down to Earth, not leaving Earth behind in order to escape to Heaven. In the same way, when we meditate we are not escaping from everyday pressures, but exploring inner possibilities so that we can bring them out into the everyday world.

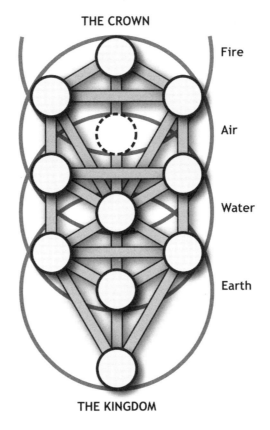

THE CROWN

Fire

Air

Water

Earth

THE KINGDOM

The Four Worlds and the Tree of Life

The Tree of Life is seen as a whole: the 'Crown' is at the top and the 'Kingdom' at the bottom, and they are reflections of each other. In the same way, our outer world – which includes our physical

Body – is a mirror image of our inner worlds. This is why it is so important to heal any mental and emotional issues that are manifesting outer problems. Often, it is easier to start from the outer edge of our Four Worlds, looking at our physical presence and what we are manifesting for ourselves and others.

Starting from the outer rim of our Four Worlds, each of the first three provides opportunities to expand our awareness and our focus from the most immediate issues to wider possibilities:

Physical World

1. Immediate personal concerns: shelter, sleeping, waking, eating, shopping
2. Extended personal concerns: career goals, financial or creative success, social status

Emotional World

3. Immediate emotional circle: personal relationships, love and harmony
4. Extended emotional circle: tolerance, empathy, compassion for all creatures

Mental World

5. Creative and intellectual mind: inspiration in arts and/or sciences
6. Visionary and prophetic mind: higher wisdom, universal love, service

Spiritual World

7. Cosmic consciousness: stillness and space – unity with the Divine

At first, we may only catch short glimpses of this beautiful state of being and it may seem difficult to integrate it with our usual everyday lives, but the more we go back to our Beloved, the more our joyful union will penetrate even the most mundane experiences.

Indian women dip white cloth in a bath of dye and spread it on their rooftops to dry in the sun. The sun bleaches out most of the colour. The cloth is dipped again and dried again, and again, and again. With each repetition, the colour becomes richer and deeper, and the sun's rays have less effect until, eventually, the colour is completely fast. Meditation is similar: as we repeatedly dip into Divine Unity, we gradually bring a richer, more reliable beam of spiritual Light into the world. As our Light beam becomes stronger, it is less likely to be diffused by worldly activities and everything we do is enriched.

Integrating your four worlds

We need to develop integrity, or wholeness, in all four areas: spiritual, mental, emotional and physical. This is the unique potential of a human being, over and above that of creatures like other animals: we have the capacity to extend our attention beyond our very personal requirements. All these possibilities are like a flower unfolding, which, when it is fully open, brings us to a great realisation, that we are not only physical animals, but also Divine. It is true that everything that exists is a manifestation of Divine Energy, but humans, as far as we know, are the only creatures on this planet who have the capacity to become consciously aware of the Divinity within.

As we open our awareness to include more possibilities, we are naturally giving space for our spiritual nature to make itself known. We are moving towards cosmic consciousness. In the state of Unity with the Divine, we become aware of the three essential qualities that underpin Creation – Power, Intelligence and Love – and we know that we can express these qualities in our everyday lives. In this state, we realise that our Guardian Angel is no longer a separate teacher and supporter, but is our 'other half'. This is what the alchemists called the 'Chymical Wedding' – the Divine Marriage. Congratulations!

Exercises: **Considering Your Four Worlds**

Physical World

1. Immediate personal concerns: shelter, sleeping, waking, eating, shopping

Consider how much time and attention you use on these daily concerns. You might like to experiment with a 'time and motion' study for a few days (a week would be best) keeping a notebook with you in order to identify how you use your time. This research will help you get an overall picture of how your 'four bodies' are functioning – are there any areas that are overemphasised? If a great deal of time is taken up with shelter (housework!), sleeping, shopping, cooking, eating and doing a job just for the money, then you might like to think how you could reorganise your timetable. As Albert Einstein said, 'To keep doing the same thing and expect a different result is the definition of insanity'.

2. Extended personal concerns: career goals, financial or creative success, social status

What are you doing that will further your personal success in the world? That might not have anything to do with financial gain, but might be a focus on becoming a better therapist or teacher. Do you have a measure of your success so far – or lack of it? Go back to your timeline and check whether there were any pointers along the route that indicate that you may have missed something important. Often – especially for women, but this can apply to men as well – we set aside dreams and visions for personal success in order to establish a sound base for our family. What are your present goals? How do they relate to the changes that are taking place in our world?

154

Any sense of insecurity or frustration hanging around immediate or extended personal concerns will make it difficult for you to feel complete and well grounded in your physical world, and will have a ripple effect on your emotional and mental worlds. If you are suffering from anxieties of this kind, feeling that you are powerless to make changes because outer circumstances seem immovable, then take up the power you do have, the power that resides in your body. Make it your focus to become healthy, strong, flexible and full of life energy. Your body is a microcosm of your world, so if your body is in great shape, everything else around you will shape up very nicely as well.

Emotional World

3. Immediate emotional circle: personal relationships, love and harmony

Take time to consider your personal relationships and the levels of beauty, love and harmony in your life. Sit with your Journal, light a candle and inwardly review the way you relate to people who play key roles in your life, whether family, friends or colleagues.

Also, during this session, think about how you support your own emotional wellbeing. What brings delight into your life? Music? Gardens? Dance? Art? The commercial world is mostly based on encouraging us to fulfil emotional needs by shopping; often, we see something, feel it will satisfy a need, buy it and then find ourselves feeling unsatisfied. Most real beauty is found in things that don't cost money, or are very low cost. Make a list of things you could bring into your life that would make you feel wonderful – but don't overstretch your credit limit.

4. Extended emotional circle: tolerance, empathy, compassion for all creatures

Take a daily newspaper and practise sending blessings to any individual or group of people who are reported as being in trouble of any kind, even if they have apparently caused the trouble for themselves. However different they are from you, however wicked they may seem to be, expand the love in your heart and reach out to them. Someone who commits murder, for example, is in great need of our compassion.

Think about animals, birds or insects that you find unpleasant or creepy and try looking at them from a new perspective. Sadly, artists through the ages have associated some creatures – snakes, toads and bats, for example – with negative potential. The snake in the Garden of Eden is the Devil in disguise, although the snake in older mystery traditions is the symbol of Wisdom. All creatures are part of the Divine plan and we need to see the *whole* of Creation as a glory, in which no single creature is lesser or greater than the rest.

Mental World
5. Creative and intellectual mind: inspiration in arts and/or sciences

Review the way in which you use your intellect – your rational mind. Do you challenge your own understanding of your mental capacity? Do you stretch what you *think* is your ability? Do you do crosswords? Do you read books that extend your knowledge? Do you set yourself tasks, such as learning a new language? How about going to a new class that covers a topic you felt weak in at school?

Make a list of possible new adventures for your mind, such as taking up chess, joining an IT course at your local college, learning a new language, finding out everything you can about a country you had never thought of visiting (maybe you will visit it before long), become a lay expert on quantum physics! Choose one of these adventures and get started. Like your body, your brain really enjoys being exercised.

6. Visionary and prophetic mind: higher wisdom, universal love, service

Expanding your mind beyond the rational allows you to connect with invisible dimensions and the beings that exist there: Angels, Archangels, guides and so on. This is the first step towards channelling messages that can support your own life and the lives of anyone you live and work with.

Meditation is the key to this expansion. Regular, twice-daily meditation will bring gradual results, but meditation retreats will accelerate the process. Most people, with families and regular work, will find it best to stick to the twice-daily routine, with occasional weekend retreats. If you cannot get away, or feel you can't afford a meditation retreat, treat yourself once a month to a quiet, introverted day, when you can fit in an extra meditation session. Here is a suggested outline for twenty-four hours, starting in the evening:

❖ Switch off all phones – make sure your friends and relatives know that you are going to be unavailable. If you have any children, or pets, arrange for someone else to look after them. If you have a partner, suggest they go off for their own special day.

❖ Throughout the day, keep your personal Journal with you, as you may well find messages or inspirations arriving and you should note them down.

The previous night
20.00   Go to bed early.

Day one
07.00   Get up. Drink a glass of hot water with lemon.

07.15   Shower. Do a few good stretches.

07.30   Twenty-minute meditation.

07.50   Write down your intentions for the coming month.

08.00   Stretching and exercising. Use simple yoga exercises or some exercise form that comes easily. Don't make it hard work. Tai chi is excellent.

08.30   Light but sustaining breakfast. A good breakfast might be porridge (made with water, not milk) served with raw honey.

09.00   Go for a brisk walk to a beautiful place. When you are there, allow yourself time to experience your surroundings, as well as some daydreaming. Walk like someone on a mission until you arrive, then find somewhere to sit undisturbed. Then walk back briskly.

10.30 Have a hot drink (but not hot chocolate or anything containing caffeine; I recommend a good-quality herbal drink). If you feel in need of a snack, eat an apple or a light cracker, such as a rice cake, rye cracker or oatcake.

11.00 Read a book you feel will help expand your mental horizons (see Recommended books, p. 223).

12.00 Eat a light lunch, something easily digestible. For example, homemade vegetable and lentil soup with oatcakes and hummus. Lentils are nourishing, oatcakes are lighter than bread, hummus is made with chick peas, which provide good protein – and using hummus means you can avoid butter (dairy products are very heavy on the digestive system).

13.00 Take a siesta! If you can't sleep, go back to your book, but put your feet up.

14.00 Do some more stretches, as at 08.00.

14.30 Thirty-minute meditation session.

15.00 More stretches, as at 08.00.

15.30 Take a hot drink, as at 10.30.

16.00 Go for another walk. Choose a change of scenery this time and just brisk walking, no daydreaming!

17.00 When you return from your walk, prepare your supper. Again, your meal should be light on the digestive system, but you could include a dessert, as long as it isn't weighed down with dairy products or wheat. Stewed fruit and non-dairy yoghurt would be suitable.

17.30 More stretches, as at 08.00.

18.00 Thirty-minute meditation.

18.30 More stretches, as at 08.00.

19.00   Eat your supper and tidy the kitchen.

20.00   More reading, while drinking a cup of chamomile or other calming or warming tea.

21.00   Have a luxurious bath, using any calming aromatherapy oils that you enjoy. (Don't wash your hair.) Afterwards, massage as much of your body as you can reach!

22.00   Do a few more stretches, just for five or ten minutes, then go to bed. You will probably be feeling mentally alert, so you might like to read some more until you are ready to drift off naturally.

Spiritual World
7. Cosmic consciousness: stillness and space – unity with the Divine

There is only one exercise that will take you there and that is meditation! It doesn't matter which technique you use, whenever your everyday chattering mind settles down into a quiet state, you open up the gateways to expanded consciousness. When you meditate, you are making Love with your Guardian Angel. This is the path to Bliss.

Visualisation: Embracing Your Beloved – At One With Your Guardian Angel, At One with Creation

❖ Once again, find yourself on that cosy sofa, gazing out into your beautiful garden. Once more, you find yourself walking out through the French windows and across the lawn, past beautiful flowers and trees until you arrive at the gate that leads you to the familiar country lane.

❖ You walk along the lane and eventually find yourself in the wood, walking on the path towards your sacred building, where the doors are open to welcome you.

❖ As you enter, the doors swing silently closed behind you and, as you move towards your special seat, you become aware of your Guardian Angel surrounding you with love.

❖ Your Guardian Angel appears as a glowing light, hovering around your head, and you realise that you are going to have a new experience. You know that all you have to do is to sit and wait.

(Short silence.)

❖ As you sit calmly waiting, you notice the light of your Guardian beginning to filter down from your head, until it seems to fill every little corner of your body. It is like a warm shower filling you with a comforting glow. The power of the light is very intense, but very loving and reassuring. You realise that this light is very familiar to you. It has always been part of you. This makes you smile and you feel like a child again.

❖ Sit quietly, breathing in the light, allowing this wonderful glow to wake up all levels of your being. It is like being in love with the most wonderful person you can think of. And you have nothing else to do but to enjoy each other's company, wrapped in your own sweet loving harmony of being.

(Short silence.)

❖ As you experience this amazing love, you discover that your thoughts are taking you on a journey. You are still wrapped up with your Guardian, it is as though you are one being and, wherever your thoughts move, your Guardian will be part of the movement.

❖ Together, as one, you move effortlessly through the ceiling of your room, so that you can look down on the woods and the top of your sacred building from a place high up in the sky. Your loving thoughts extend outwards to include everything you can see: the green trees below; the birds in the sky; the snowy mountaintops in the distance. Now you are moving over the sea, watching flying fish and dolphins leaping. All of them are in your heart. Your love has no boundaries and you find yourself diving to the bottom of the ocean, seeing strange creatures and mysterious reefs. Then you move upwards again until you find yourself among the stars of the Milky Way and your mind stretches out to include the galaxies. Now you know that you are one with every part of Creation and that your own thoughts are helping to create this beauty and wonder.

❖ Gradually, your thoughts gently turn towards returning home. You are looking for planet Earth and for the woods that protect your sacred building. When you can see the top of your building, you descend very softly, back through the ceiling to find your seat once more.

❖ You still have the sense of being at one with your Guardian. Sit quietly, breathing deeply, as you recall the warm love of your Beloved.

(Short silence.)

❖ Now rise from your seat and walk towards the door of your sacred building, still feeling the oneness with your Guardian. As you walk through the woods, along the country lane and back through the garden gate, you can still feel this sensation. Your Guardian is not just with you – your Guardian is part of you.

❖ You find yourself back in the sitting room and make your way to the sofa. Sit there quietly for a moment, allowing the new feeling of being at one with your Guardian to stay with you.

❖ Now, very gradually, bring yourself back to the present reality. Take extra time to come back, so that you do not lose this new feeling.

Mandy worked with this visualisation during my eClass and afterwards shared her inspiring story:

MANDY'S EXPERIENCE

At first, I thought that nothing much had changed, but a week later I was drinking my cup of tea and relaxing, and I started thinking about what will happen when (or if) my company sacks me, how I will manage and so on.

Suddenly, I became really angry with this 'Doubting Jane' residing in me and found myself shouting at 'her' to get out, telling her that I did not need her. In my mind, I saw a long stick with a huge foot at the end kicking Doubting Jane into a deep well – so deep she could never get out.

When Jane had been kicked into the well, I saw that behind her was another me – 'Everyday Mandy' – curled up under a table, hiding as though she was scared. I asked her to come out, but she just shook her head and said, 'No', because she was frightened. I sent her healing with the colour of pink, for love, and then she came out and opened up like the petals of a flower. I hugged this 'Loving Mandy' and turned around to introduce her to our Guardian Angel, who had been standing patiently near by. He came to us and we hugged each other and, as we hugged, 'Loving Mandy' and I became one. Our Angel continued hugging me and kept on giving me love and protection, saying that he was always there for me and I had nothing to fear. As he talked, he too started merging into me and I felt a warm glow inside bursting with love, warmth and light. My Guardian was also a part of me now.

Since that day, this feeling of fear as to what will happen has gone. Instead, I know something wonderful is going to happen to me and I just can't wait!

Mandy's story also reminds us that the effects of our inner work do not always happen instantaneously but, when we relax and allow the process to unfold, we may be surprised.

There are several important ingredients that will help us relax and will make all the difference to our spiritual progress. Think TALL ...

T = Trust
A = Ask
L = Listen
L = Love

and you can add two more 'L's for good Luck ... **L**ive and **L**augh!

Trust is the first step – the rest follow easily when trust is in place. Trust is not just a mental 'belief'; it is a state of peace and at-oneness with the Divine, the oneness we feel when we are in the very deepest state of meditation. Then we are at ease with our Guardian Angel and we are no longer anxious, frustrated or overwhelmed by everyday stress. In that deep state of peace we are like children. We have surrendered all our anxieties and we are allowing Divine Love to fill every cell of our body. This innocence allows manifestation to unfold without the restrictions of our usual concerns. Too often we think, 'I need this' or, 'I want that', and we say to ourselves, 'How can it come to me; I don't understand "how" this can happen?' But the Divine Source doesn't worry about 'how' to create, It just wills something to occur and there, like magic, it arrives.

14

Travelling to Celestial Realms

Upon seraph wings of ecstasy . . .
He pass'd the flaming bounds of place and time:
The living throne, the sapphire blaze,
Where angels tremble, while they gaze . . .

THOMAS GRAY

Exploring inner kingdoms

The inner journey towards cosmic consciousness – towards the 'Divine Marriage' with our Guardian Angel – brings us to a sense of completeness within ourselves and with the world. This journey takes us through many unfolding layers or levels of consciousness, during which we uncover the nature of our own Soul. On the way, we travel through invisible dimensions where we may encounter celestial beings. Carl Jung said that the new exploration for humanity was not 'outer space' but 'inner space'. And our inner space contains all those dimensions that were described by the old mystics. When we go beyond the narrow focus of our personality, which is an essential tool for functioning in the world, we can voyage to many different realms and commune with guides and celestial beings, including Angels, Archangels, Seraphim and so on. These 'beings' do not have physical bodies, but we can 'see' them and experience their presence through our visionary 'eyes'. When someone asks me, 'How do I know this is a real experience, not just my imagination?' I explain that the imagination is our most powerful tool in our spiritual development – it is not 'just' imagination. It allows us to process and shape our inner experiences so that we can reach an understanding that will be helpful to us.

Imagine you were in a cinema and the screen was dark. Then you hear someone speaking and you have the vague impression that they are telling a story, but they are speaking in another language so you don't understand anything. Part of you is wishing for some subtitles or pictures, so that you can make sense of the information. In a similar way, your mind reaches into the deep space of consciousness where there are many layers of information – a treasury of wisdom – but you have no way to access or understand it. This is where your imagination becomes your interpreter, creating the visions that bring the jewels of wisdom into your consciousness.

Much of the wisdom we can access has been embedded deep in Creation since time began. The structures of Creation are like the architecture in a great cathedral and the angelic hosts are the pillars and buttresses. But there are also layers of accumulated wisdom that have been collected during the lives of our ancestors, both ancient and modern. So, as well as communing with angelic beings, we can have conversations with the elders and spiritual guardians of the human race.

The mystics used 'maps' of the spiritual worlds in order to create markers, just as a guide taking you into the jungle might do. Inner space, like outer space, is infinite, so it is very helpful to learn from those who have gone before us. The Four Worlds, which I described in Chapter 13, is one of the most helpful maps that I have worked with. It demonstrates the way in which the creative energy of the Divine Spirit unfolds in a series of layers and how a chain of celestial supporters or assistants develops, in order to expand and sustain creative possibilities.

The original idea that stimulates Creation can be likened to the Big Bang: some enormous power is driving the beginning of something new that has yet to unfold. We can call this power the Creator, God, Divine Source or, as the mediaeval mystics would say, the *Primum Mobile* – the First Mover. The element of Fire represents the first 'movement' – the spiritual passion and drive that initiates the process.

So what is the second 'movement'? After the Big Bang comes the first stage of cooling, when gases start to form. In the Four Worlds model, the element of Air represents the mental process of planning and organising. Think of an artist or writer who might have a brilliant fiery flash of inspiration for their next creative project – how consuming that vision can be! But nothing will develop from that Fire unless some cool thinking and consideration takes place. A writer will have to make a book plan, decide how many words and chapters to write, create an outline plot and so on.

After the cooling creates gases, we have the possibility of that life-enhancing, life-sustaining by-product – water. The third-stage element of Water represents our feelings and emotions, and the artist or author needs to be sustained by positive feelings and a sense of self-worth. Just as water nurtures the baby in the womb, the creative product also needs nurturing in the form of loving attention and commitment – these will be the greatest contribution to the final completion of the project. All the passion of Fire and intellect of Air will come to nothing unless someone is looking after the unborn baby.

Think of a plant. It needs water, but it also requires good nutrients – without these, it will wither and die. Similarly, in human life, the Water represents loving attention, but nutrients are also needed. These include the practical necessities that keep us going – resources that support our wellbeing, such as food, shelter and money. The artist has her inspiration (Fire), she has planned her project (Air), she has her paints and canvas, and has the time set aside (Water), but now she actually has to start painting. If this

166

process is followed through with determination and commitment, then the fourth stage comes together naturally: the 'baby' of our creative vision will be born as a matter of course.

When all four 'movements' or stages have unfolded, the creation is complete – the inspiration, the planning and the loving care have brought the project to birth. It has developed from a vision to a reality – it has come to Earth. But the final result must never lose touch with the processes that brought it into manifestation, otherwise its reason for being will be sacrificed and it will not be sustained for very long. We are committed to repeating the cycle – honouring the results of our visions, but moving on. We limit our possibilities if we hover too long in the fourth world, congratulating ourselves on our results, or clinging on to them in case we lose them. We see from this model that everything that happens in our lives can be described in these four stages.

Celestial supporters

The mystics taught that at each stage the Creator would extend or disperse power to celestial beings that could assist in the various stages:

The Seraphim exist in the First World of Fire. The Hebrew word *sarap* means 'to burn'. In the vision of Isaiah, they are singing, 'Holy, Holy, Holy'; I think of them as cheerleaders, fanning the fires of our passion.

The Archangels exist in the Second World of Air. They are the airy organisers and planners who focus the different tasks that need to be carried out. They don't *do* anything, they just *think* about doing things and describe how they should be done. If the Creator is the patron of a grand new building project, the Archangels are the designers, each in charge of a different aspect of the project. And, just as in a building project, there would be different skilled organisers required, such as a Master Stonemason, a Master Electrician and a Master Plumber, so each Archangel is only in charge of one area of Creation.

167

The Angels exist in the Third World of Water. It might seem strange to associate them with this element, after all they are not mermaids or dolphins. But Water represents feelings and emotions, and this World is where our project is nurtured. Care and attention are essential, so the vision does not lose momentum. The job of the Angels is to take care of your needs, bringing together the right people and resources, and providing emotional support.

The nature spirits and elementals exist in the Fourth World of Earth, busy alongside us humans. Planet Earth is a project that has been unfolding for millions of years and we all need to honour it. Within our dimension, we can also find the spirits of our ancestors – humans who no longer live on our plane of existence, but whose wisdom is available to us if we choose to ask.

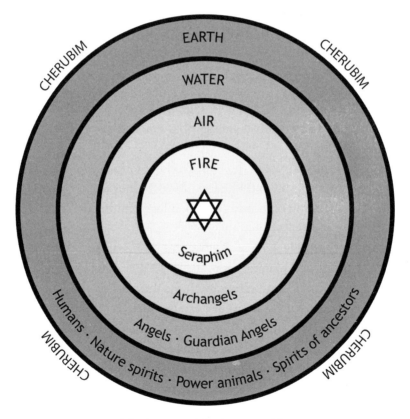

The beings of the Four Worlds

Cherubim

The Cherubim belong in the mysterious 'fifth element' – the *quinta essentia* or *anima mundi* (Soul of the world) – an overarching element that glues everything together. They watch over all four stages and elements of Creation. This is why they have been seen in visions with four faces – Lion, Man, Eagle and Bull – representing the four fixed signs of the zodiac:

Animal	Zodiac Sign	Element
Lion	Leo	Fire
Man	Aquarius	Air
Eagle	Scorpio	Water
Bull	Taurus	Earth

As you journey inwards through these four levels towards the meeting with your Soul, you may encounter any or all of these amazing beings and you can ask for their support.

Physical world – humans, power animals, spirits of ancestors, Nature spirits

As soon as you embark on your quest for wholeness, you can ask for support and guidance from helpers in any of the Four Worlds, although it is good to start in the Earth World, as you are less likely to have problems staying grounded. People who are not grounded find that otherworldly connections make it difficult for them to get on with everyday tasks and they may become rather dreamy or disconnected. Also, if you want to develop confidence gradually, it is often best to work at a level that is familiar to you, whether this is with the spirit of someone you know who has died, with a nature spirit in your garden or with a power animal that might be represented by your own pet. For a spiritual guide, you might prefer to talk to someone you knew about because of your family religion – a teacher, saint or prophet, perhaps.

Often, people will start thinking about spiritual matters when someone in the family dies and they get the impression that their loved one is still around. This feeling may prompt a visit to a Spiritualist Church, where spiritual mediums offer to make connections with dead spirits. Although this may be helpful, I should warn you that people who have died don't necessarily have the capacity to offer any more wisdom than they would have done when they were alive.

Like other guides, a helper in the shape of a power animal can present itself in a dream. When he was at Cambridge University, the poet, Ted Hughes, dreamed that a fiery fox came into his room. He was studying Literature and had been struggling with a critical essay. The dream fox stood on its hind legs and placed its paw on the essay. Then it announced, 'This is killing us'. So the future poet laureate changed his subject to Anthropology because he realised that analysing other people's poetry was destructive to his own creative possibilities and interfered with his intuitive talent.

My husband Will had a series of dreams about a black panther, during which he became progressively less and less afraid of this usually scary animal. He felt it was telling him to take up his own powerful possibilities. At this time we didn't have a cat in our household – Will was not very fond of them – but the dream turned around his attitude. After the last dream, in which the wild panther had become his friend, he announced that if he could find a black kitten, he would be delighted to have a cat in our house. The very same morning, he took our daughter to nursery and saw a notice offering kittens free to good homes. 'Have you got a perfectly plain black one,' he asked, 'with absolutely no sign of any white on it?' As you may guess, the answer was yes. That was how Pluto, the cat from the underworld, came into our lives.

I have already told you how Pythagoras spoke to me during a meditation – this is a good example of guidance from a spiritual ancestor – and in the next chapter I will explain how, more recently,

I started talking to the Nephalim. You can ask to meet any spiritual master or mistress that you choose. Once you are practised at turning inwards using your favourite meditation technique, just ask!

It is easy to commune with Nature spirits and elementals, especially in places of natural beauty. Even if you only have access to Nature in a nearby park or in pots on your patio, you can sit quietly and allow these magical beings to make their presence felt.

Here are some suggestions for working with helpers in this World:

Power animals

Working with power animals is a big topic and has been covered very well by other writers. If you want to work in this way, look out for the *Medicine Cards* set by David Carson and Jamie Sams (see Recommended books, p. 223). The beautiful images and stories are a good starting place.

❖ Experiment by choosing a single card from the *Medicine Cards* set each day, standing it up in front of you while you meditate, or putting it under your pillow at night. Start at the beginning of the pack, making no judgement about which animal might be 'right' or 'wrong' for you. Keep your Journal near by so that you can make notes of your experiences.

Spiritual guides and ancestors

If you want to contact a relative who has recently died, such as a grandparent, or someone you feel could offer you wise guidance, then one possibility is to go to a Spiritualist Church. However, I think it is kindest to our deceased loved ones to let them carry on with their own process on 'the other side'. By calling on them for help, we could be hindering their own development. I suggest you ask for guidance from one of the great elders who have already committed to helping humanity.

Choose a spiritual teacher you believe was a good person who offered humanity wisdom of the highest order when they were alive. Be very selective – some of the currently popular 'Ascended Masters' were not particularly wise when they were alive. For example, Count St Germain was regarded as a fraud in his lifetime and a mythology has grown around him which doesn't seem to be justified by any of the facts. He certainly didn't leave a legacy of wise sayings or parables that can help us in our lives. Find out what you can about any teacher you might feel called to work with and decide for yourself. Reading their handed-down wisdom creates a good connection for you; you will already feel you know something about them before you ask for help. Of course, they might start the conversation themselves if there is something in you that is on their wavelength. When I met Pythagoras, I had never come across his wise sayings, *The Golden Verses of Pythagoras*, but I very soon found them (see Recommended books, p. 223). Think about it like this: if you were going to purchase an expensive antique chair you would want to know its 'provenance' – the seller should be able to provide evidence that the chair is a real antique, not a copy, or a fake. Whenever you come across interesting ideas, or hear about helpful guides, ask yourself where did these ideas come from? Who was this person when they were alive? Who has written this book? Where did the author hear about this? If it is 'channelled', can I trust the person who is channelling? You can easily get misled by cheap imitations unless you use your critical abilities!

❖ When you feel ready, set up a special meditation session and ask your chosen teacher to make their presence felt. If this doesn't happen straight away, be patient. Sometimes, guides turn up when you have moved your attention elsewhere and have stopped looking out for them in a state of urgency. Mystical experiences and openings to other dimensions happen most easily when you are in a state of restful alertness – prepared, but not desperate.

Nature spirits

In order to connect with these elusive helpers, you need a great deal of patience, as well as the ability to be very still and unobtrusive. Their real task is not to help humanity but to maintain the natural world.

When I was a young girl, I lived in an isolated rural area and I was very keen to see the fairies. On my long, solitary walks in the countryside I would feel their magic around me, like a kind of buzzing. On spring and summer nights, when there was a full moon, I would climb out of my bedroom window (we lived in a bungalow) and tiptoe across the lawn, hoping to see the fairies. I never saw a single one! In fact, in all the years I have been working with the Angels, I hadn't seen a fairy until, a couple of years ago. I was giving a Shefa workshop in a magical Welsh valley, where a lovely French lady I know, Veronique, teaches Reiki and Munay Ki. Many places in Wales are untouched and you can still feel the deep, ancient magic of Nature and this one made me catch my breath when I arrived. There is a beautiful stream running by the old mill where Veronique teaches and where I was holding the class. One afternoon, I glanced out of the window and caught a fleeting glimpse of a being that was larger than a butterfly, but smaller than any bird in this country. It was translucent and shimmering in the sunlight. Then, like a flash it was gone. The gossamer-light fairies and their elvish friends don't have much time for us – they are much too busy.

If you are working with Nature, perhaps in a garden, or if you regularly visit botanical gardens, you may be surprised by an unexpected visitor. In *The Findhorn Garden Story* (see Recommended books, p. 223), Robert Ogilvie Crombie describes how he met Pan, the God of Nature, in the Botanical Gardens in Edinburgh. The early Findhorn Community were in regular communion with nature spirits, who advised them how to make the best use of the sandy soil – this helped them to grow forty-pound cabbages!

❖ Find a local beauty spot – somewhere with running water would be a good choice. Identify a place where you can go regularly, where you can sit quietly without being disturbed. Sit down, preferably on the ground but, if it is wet, you may need a blanket. Sitting directly on the ground will put you in touch with Mother Earth.

❖ Sit for a few moments in silent meditation with your eyes closed. Ask in your mind to see a Nature spirit. Then open your eyes, but stay in a meditative state – not trying hard, but just allowing your senses to pick up any presences.

❖ Be prepared to be still and quiet for a long time. Be patient and humble – be prepared to go back on many occasions. Don't *try* to see anything. Relax and feel yourself in contact with the natural surroundings, allowing your everyday thoughts to drift.

I can't guarantee that you will see anything (although you may experience a presence in another way, such as a movement in the air around you or a high-pitched noise), but I am sure you will gradually feel closer to the natural world and this will help you in many ways. You may find the spontaneous healing of minor problems takes place and you will certainly feel more relaxed in your everyday 'busy-ness'.

Emotional world – your Guardian Angel and other Angels

The most important Angel from this world is your Guardian Angel, but you can also ask for support from other Angels, either directly or by asking your Guardian Angel to draw their help towards you. The Angels in this world do not have names; you could describe them as networkers, creating necessary links between people, nudging us to do certain things when we don't quite know why, just so we will meet a the right person, pick up a particular book or turn down a different road. I also think of them as behind-the-scenes organisers, like stage managers or dressers in the theatre. These unseen workers provide the back-up for the performers so that the right costume or prop is always where it should be at exactly the right time. This helps to make the show seem effortless to the audience, who only see what is on the stage.

Here are some suggestions for working with Angels:

❖ Think of something you are hoping to bring into your life – an event or a project you would like to create – for which you need some help. Now take another journey to talk to your Guardian Angel (see p. 67).

❖ While you are in your sacred space with your Guardian Angel beside you, visualise the event or project, as you want it to be. Think about the various things that need doing and ask your Guardian to help you attract some Angels to help with each task. For example, you might be organising a big birthday event for an elderly family member. You need transport, a venue, a source of china, tablecloths and cutlery, a good cake baker, a florist and a great outfit to wear.

❖ Ask for an Angel to help with each separate topic – that's the way they work best. Visualise them all hovering around you, waiting for instructions. You could imagine giving them each a piece of card with your order written on it. Ask them to help you bring all these things together quickly, easily and within budget.

❖ Say 'thank you' in advance, because you know they will sort everything out for you.

❖ Imagine them zipping away, leaving you with your Guardian Angel. Ask your Guardian to keep an eye on progress, while you are busy in your everyday world. Then say 'thank you' again before you leave.

Whenever requesting angelic help with manifestation, you need to stay alert for signs. Obviously, if you are planning a party, you are the one who will have to phone the venue and make the booking. But with angelic help you are likely to have the venue brought to your attention, perhaps in a casual conversation with someone, or you *just happen* to see a card in a shop window, one that you don't usually go to but which you *just happen* to have visited. There are lots of *'just happen'* occasions when you have asked for angelic help. But you do have to pay attention and pick up the subtle hints that arrive – sometimes just a passing thought can send you in a better direction, as long as you don't override the thought because it doesn't seem 'sensible'.

Mental world – Archangels: creative architects who help you to redesign your life

Archangels are found in the next world up from the Angels, although their worlds are always overlapping, like a series of links in a chain. We know when an Angel is an Archangel, because it has a name. Nearly all of their names are Hebrew and they usually end with *el* (meaning 'of God'), while the first part of the name usually indicates the Archangel's role in the creative process. Raphael, for example, means 'Healer of God', because *raph* is Hebrew for 'healing'. In the famous *Dictionary of Angels* (see Recommended books, p. 223) there are many, many Archangels, so you need to choose the most suitable ones for your purposes.

Why would you choose to work with Archangels, rather than Angels? The Angels deal with small, everyday issues, whereas the Archangels can help you to restructure or plan your life choices at a more fundamental level. They also support different qualities, as you can see from the table below. For example, if you want to develop more courage – perhaps you need to stand up for something you believe in – you would work with Michael. If you need to develop your communications skills – say, to improve your public speaking skills – then Gabriel is the Archangel you need to call on.

Many New Age teachers work with the famous seven Archangels that are found in old Christian texts (the Roman Catholic Church only recognises the first three because they are the only ones mentioned in the Bible and the Apocrypha):

- ❖ Michael

- ❖ Raphael

- ❖ Gabriel

- ❖ Uriel

- ❖ Cassiel

- ❖ Chamuel

- ❖ Jophiel

I would expect people who have chosen to offer service for the benefit of humanity to have the support of an Archangel, in addition to that of their Guardian Angel. For example, healers often acknowledge that Raphael seems to come automatically into their consciousness when they are giving healing.

For many years I have worked with my own Archangel, who I asked to accompany me when I chose my present life, but I have also worked with the twelve Archangels of the Tree of Life, who are often called the Guardians of the Gates of Light. I made contact with them in the early '80s, after having a vision of Sandalphon during a meditation. To remind you of these Archangels' names, here is the Tree of Life diagram again (you will notice that some of their names match the list of seven Archangels in the previous list above).

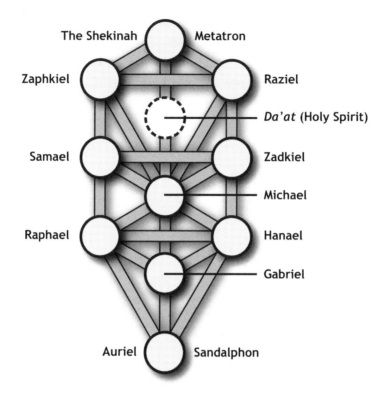

The Shekinah • Metatron
Zaphkiel • Raziel
Da'at (Holy Spirit)
Samael • Zadkiel
Michael
Raphael • Hanael
Gabriel
Auriel • Sandalphon

The Archangels of the Tree of Life

In Appendix 3 (p. 215) there is a table showing the qualities of the Archangels, but if you want to work in depth with these awesome powers, I suggest you read my book, *Working with Archangels* (see Theolyn's books, p. 221). In the meantime, here is a suggestion for working with Sandalphon and Auriel. These two Archangels reside at the foot of the Tree of Life and are good companions during our in-the-body experience as human beings, offering us down-to-earth companionship and tender loving care.

❖ Create a sacred space using a beautiful cloth, some crystals, flowers, candles and incense (frankincense would be suitable for Sandalphon and jasmine for Auriel). Think about the qualities and key words for the Archangels when you choose these items:

Sandalphon – trust, reliability, stewardship; Auriel – salvation, tender loving care, spiritual grace, mending hurts.

❖ You could write these key words in beautiful handwriting on some special card, then cut this into small pieces, with one word on each piece. Spread the words around your sacred space. These preparations allow your consciousness to start calling the Archangels towards you, even before you have started meditating. While you are organising your sacred space, you can consider the help or advice you would like from the Archangels. If you want to see some images of Sandalphon and Auriel, go to my website (www.theolyn.com).

❖ You can use music if you wish. I know people find music helps them to relax, but it does also mean that part of the mind is occupied with processing the experience of listening, so it can distract from a pure experience.

❖ Take yourself on the inner journey to visit your Guardian Angel in your sacred space. While you are sitting peacefully with your Guardian, ask if you can be introduced to Sandalphon and Auriel. Your Guardian will accompany you towards a gateway made of light and, as you pass through the gate, you will feel the presence of these two beautiful Archangels.

❖ Take your time, as long as you wish, to ask for any help and guidance you feel you need.

❖ When you are ready to return, say thank you and ask your Guardian Angel to take you home. Make sure you are well grounded, stretching your limbs, wriggling your hands and feet and tapping your body.

You can make a return journey at any time.

Spiritual world – Seraphim: cheerleaders who keep your inner fire alight

The fiery Seraphim are so close to the Divine Source that we can hardly think of them with our everyday minds. How can we warm ourselves by their fire, so that we are filled with passion and inspiration? Meditation is the key to returning to the First World. There are no words or visualisations that can take us there, just a letting-go process by which we release ourselves from the constraints of time and space and expand our consciousness beyond the limits of thought, feelings and physicality. Many people who say they cannot settle down to meditate, because their mind is so crowded with everyday thoughts, find mantra meditation very helpful. (You can buy the powerful *Simple Meditation* technique as a CD or MP3 (see Theolyn's CDs, p. 222).

Here are some suggestions for working with the Seraphim:

❖ Find the best meditation technique for yourself. You will know if your meditation is working because you will find your body becoming very still and your thoughts will settle down until, on some occasions, you might realise that you haven't been thinking at all. Sometimes, you will notice a sensation of golden light filling your head and spreading around your body. When your individual 'I' melts into the great 'I AM' of unified consciousness, your whole body is filled with light, and many troubles, whether emotional or physical, can be healed.

❖ The following visualisation has been created to help you move beyond the Earth plane and experience the other three Worlds. Maybe you will catch a glimpse of the Seraphim:

Visualisation: **The Heavenly Halls**

❖ As you breathe in and out deeply and slowly, allow your mind to take you back to the familiar sitting room. Take your usual journey through the garden, along the country lane, into the quiet woods where your sacred building opens its doors to welcome you.

❖ As you sit on your special seat, the doors to your building close softly. This time, you realise that your Guardian Angel is not a separate presence, but shines like a light inside you. This makes you smile with delight. You sit there for a moment, enjoying the sensation of being at one with your Guardian.

❖ Now you decide that you want to take another journey. You have chosen to meet the celestial beings that support Creation and are waiting for the first sign so your journey can begin.

❖ The ceiling above your head seems to be singing and, as you watch, it melts away so all you can see are many coloured lights, twinkling like stars. You find yourself lifted up and up, into a beautiful hall with a golden floor. The twinkling lights surround you. There are many glowing spheres, orbs of light that move from place to place so quickly that you can hardly count them. You realise that these are Angels and you watch them as they stream their light across the area above your head, making lines of light that join, then turn, then join again. You hardly know where to look next. You have no bodily sensation, just a feeling of joy and wonder brimming within your heart.

❖ Now the Angels seem to be singing, 'Come with us' …

❖ … and you find yourself walking across a pavement made of crystal towards a shining palace, where the doors and windows glow like jewels.

❖ As you enter the palace hall, you gaze at the amazing windows, where the coloured lights create images of the mighty Archangels. You can see Michael with his breastplate glowing like the Sun and he calls to you. His voice is like a roll of thunder, echoing across a valley:

❖ 'You are welcome to the Hall of the Archangels and your pure intent will open your heart to the wisdom we have to offer. You can come here whenever you choose, to seek help and advice.'

❖ You look around the Hall and notice other well-known Archangels: Raphael, Gabriel, Auriel and many others. You understand that you have access to their power whenever you need support.

❖ The singing is growing louder and you find yourself moving upwards again, towards a window in the roof of the palace. You are lifted through the window and find yourself in another hall, so large that you cannot see the edges. The crystal light reflects back at you and you are almost blinded, like being in bright sunshine when new snow is all around.

❖ You hear voices singing, 'Holy, Holy, Holy' ... and you know that you are in the presence of the Seraphim. Allow the Holy power of the Divine to fill you now and every day.

❖ Gradually, you find yourself sinking downwards, leaving the Hall of the Seraphim until you are back in the Hall of Archangels. These great beings shine in the window spaces as you descend even further, down into the Hall of Angels, where the orbs of light are still moving at high speed. You feel their love and their commitment to creating harmony.

❖ Now you descend further until you find yourself back on the seat in your sacred room and, as you watch, the ceiling closes above your head.

❖ Sit quietly for a moment while you recall this amazing journey. You know that, whenever you wish, you can visit those Heavenly Halls again for loving support, advice and knowledge.

(Short silence.)

❖ Now get up from your seat and walk towards the door, which opens so that you can see the path that leads back to your house. As you walk through the wood and along the country lane, you can still feel your Guardian Angel like a light inside you.

❖ You are walking through the garden, back through the French windows and now you sit down on the sofa, which is waiting for you.

My students always report beautiful and inspiring experiences when they use this visualisation.

NINA'S EXPERIENCE

When I first started to look up at the ceiling, I saw it was covered with beautiful ivy. Later, I found out that ivy is symbolic of the journey of the Soul and the spiral towards the self. It was just amazing! The ceiling disappeared and I was lifted upwards. In some way, I could not feel my body, I just felt like a ray of light. The Hall of Angels was full of these wonderful orbs of light, crystals everywhere, and I could see a bright blue light fill the hall. I don't know what this means, but it was beautiful, together with the bright light from the Angels. When I entered the Hall of Archangels, I felt humble and joyful at the same time. Archangel Michael was welcoming me. Though I couldn't see him, I felt his presence, his shining light. I felt the light and the presence of the other Archangels as well. So much light and compassion. The journey continued to the enormous Hall of the Seraphim.

All this beautiful bright light surrounded me while I was hearing Theolyn's soft voice saying, 'Allow this Holy power of the Divine to fill you now and every day.'

I could hear myself saying, 'Yes'.

VERONIQUE'S EXPERIENCE

When in the Hall of the Angels, I felt that I could have stayed there for longer and, once I was close to the Seraphim, it felt as if my body no longer existed. At the same time, I felt a great heat in and around me. It was as if every one of my cells had had 'central heating' installed in them. Although I wanted to get closer to the Seraphim and stay in contact for longer than the visualisation allowed, I was told by my Guardian Angel that one needed to be ready (energy-wise) to be able to sustain a closer approach to these great beings of light. I guess that meant my energy field needed to be vibrating at a higher rate in order to be close to such intense light.

Veronique was quite right – we do need to raise the rate of our vibrations in order to access the more subtle dimensions in the Four Worlds. Raising our vibrations happens easily when we meditate: change to a simple diet, focus on positive possibilities and keep ourselves physically fit.

15

The Return of the Nephalim

… when the sons of God came in unto the daughters of men, and they bare children unto them, the same became the mighty men which were of old, men of renown.

GENESIS 6 4

How I received messages from the Nephalim

In January 2009, just as I was going to sleep one night, I had a beautiful vision of a luminous dove that seemed to be beckoning me towards a portal. It was rather like the classic near-death experience, when people see a tunnel with a light at the end.

Through the other side of the portal I had a glimpse of several men and women, whose faces were glowing, radiant and majestic. They beckoned me forward. They were not Angels or Archangels, but seemed to be in a different class altogether. I was told they would give me messages at a later date. I was pleased there would be a time delay on more information, as I felt totally overawed and wasn't sure that I could take in much more at the time. The whole experience literally took my breath away. I lay in my bed for a couple of hours, trying to bring myself back to my body.

Over the next few days, many thoughts about the meaning and symbolism in the vision started to rush into my mind and I noticed several signs of confirmation. The first morning after my encounter with the dove, an advertising flyer came through my door, asking for clothing for third-world countries. The leaflet showed a white dove flying across a sky-blue background. In the afternoon, I walked into a nearby busy shopping mall and noticed a dove imprinted into a steel plate set into the pavement in Dove Alley. Most probably, I had walked over it many times before and never noticed it. A week later, I heard that the BBC was organising choirs around the country to record 'Oh for the Wings of a Dove' in celebration of the two hundredth anniversary of the birth of the composer, Felix Mendelssohn. So I knew that the sign was not just a personal sign but a 'wonder' as well – indicating something of wider import than my personal spiritual growth.

Although I often receive messages from 'upstairs' for myself and my clients, I hadn't received any substantial material (the kind that needs to be shared among larger groups of people) since 1994, when I had channelled the messages for *The Angels Script* (see Theolyn's books, p. 221). I felt out of practice and very busy. But over the following twelve months, I gave short bursts of time (when they nagged me) to transcribe messages delivered by twelve discarnate beings – six 'men' and six 'women' calling themselves Nephalim.

Who are the Nephalim?

The book of *Genesis* in the Bible tells us that in ancient times there was a race of tall people, giants, called Nephalim. They are described as the 'great heroes of old', who were the children of the *bene elohim* (the sons of God, usually thought of as Angels) and human women. We can read the names of several generations of remarkable men, beginning with Seth, who was one of the sons of

Adam. They all lived amazingly long lives, from over three hundred to nearly a thousand years. One of the descendants of Seth was Noah and the *Book of Enoch* describes him being born with white hair, white skin and shining eyes, so that his father wondered whether he was an Angel. Although we have no archaeological evidence to support the biblical story, there are very ancient statues and clay tablets, dating back nearly five thousand years, depicting people with very large eyes who certainly look like otherworldly beings (see Christian and Barbara O'Brien's *The Shining Ones* – Recommended books, p. 223).

The apocryphal text called the *Book of Enoch*, which was not included in the Bible, suggests that the Angels who came down to bed the 'daughters of men' were wicked Angels. These so-called 'fallen' Angels introduced humans to all kinds of advanced skills, such as metallurgy and cosmology and, because we were too naive to know how to handle these gifts, we abused the power that the Angels had given us, in defiance of God.

The word *nephal* is difficult to translate. It could mean 'to fall' and this may have led to the idea that the Nephalim were the children of 'fallen' Angels, but some scholars suggest they were given this title because their appearance caused people to fall down in amazement. This would not be surprising if they were angelic giants! *Nephal* is also the Aramaic word for the constellation Orion and this suggests that the Angels who came to Earth may have been extraterrestrials. However, none of these old stories can be verified, and it doesn't help our spiritual development to fantasise. All we can do is consider whether these invisible helpers have any wisdom to offer us.

At this point, perhaps I should mention my own thoughts about 'fallen' or 'dark' Angels. The short answer is I don't believe in them. The Book of Enoch was not translated into English until 1821, but the ideas in it had already filtered into popular thinking, partly because the story of the battle in Heaven, in which Michael defeats Satan, is included in the New Testament Book of Revelation. This is where most modern Christians have heard about the idea of 'fallen' Angels.

I have two reasons for not believing in 'fallen' Angels. The first is logical: Angels have no free will and therefore have no possibility of rebelling. They have been put in their place by the Divine Intelligence behind Creation and, unlike human beings, they just get on with the job they have been given, without any possibility of deviating from their appointed purpose. The second reason I believe the idea of 'fallen' Angels is unhelpful is that I see the movement between so-called 'light' and 'dark' as a necessary part of the creative process, not a battleground. For instance, plants need to lose their flowers and die down to create compost for new seedlings to appear; younger generations need to overturn older social structures in order to make room for new, fresh ideas that revitalise our culture; human beings need to die in order to make room for new life, and in order to experience spiritual re-birth. In addition, we are all aware that there are many shades of grey between the extremes of 'light' and 'dark' and we cannot label everything that is difficult or challenging as 'evil'. Often, that which is most challenging contains the greatest possibility for self-development.

The Enochian texts are based on a dualistic theology, in which there are two opposing forces at work – 'Good' versus 'Evil'. The idea that there is an 'evil' force, constantly attempting to corrupt humanity, seems to be stuck in our collective psychology and has provided writers with dramatic plots for many great tales, from Milton's *Paradise Lost*, to J.K. Rowling's *Harry Potter* series. Believing that 'evil' is at large in our world gives us the feeling that we are 'good', while others are 'evil'. This allows us to think that 'bad' things only happen because of some external force, which is beyond our control. The myth of 'evil' provokes world leaders and tabloid newspapers to point fingers at other nations, or individuals with anti-social tendencies, and label them as less than human. This way of thinking encourages us to blame 'dark forces' for 'negative' actions and this seems to me to be an evasion of our responsibilities. Most of the horrible things that happen on Earth are due to human stupidity, laziness, ignorance or wickedness. We can't blame 'fallen Angels' or 'demons' for our own bad behaviour.

Early biblical texts describe a God who is in charge of *both* sides of Creation: 'I form the light and create darkness, I bring prosperity and create disaster; I, the Lord, do all these things' (*Isaiah* 45:7). This more holistic version of the Divine relationship with humans allows us to see that success and failure, joy and sorrow, and all the other ups and downs, are part of a whole and are not the result of two competing powers. We can also appreciate that our positive relationship with the creative power of the universe will lead to harmony and we do not need to fear a legion of wicked Angels who are trying to drag us down! I have come across a website that is spreading the idea that the return of the Nephalim is a sign that the wicked Angels are back. I do not believe that the Nephalim are to be feared, although they were obviously truly amazing. If you take some time to meditate and ask for advice from the Nephalim I have been talking to, then I am quite sure you will receive wise advice from these gracious supporters of humanity.

A positive message from the Nephalim

The spokesperson for the group I have been communicating with is called Seth and he describes the Nephalim as half Angel, half human. Seth explained to me that they incarnated on Earth in order to help humans live up to their divine possibilities. This descent was not based on a rebellion or a wish to challenge the Divine, but rather to support humanity so that we could evolve rapidly towards a state of cosmic consciousness. According to several ancient myths, human beings at that time did not live up to this invitation and many regions of the Earth were flooded. This was not the 'punishment' of a wrathful God, but an inevitable result of trying to live on the Earth without due respect for the natural order.

Seth represents a particular group of Nephalim; he tells me there are many, many more Nephalim who are discarnate, and that there are also Nephalim who have recently incarnated and are alive on planet Earth at this present time. Some might be in the public eye, but many are just getting on with their service to humanity in quiet and unobtrusive ways. Seth says they are here to support us during the years ahead as we move into our divine possibilities:

> We are not a council of instructors or masters, we cannot solve your problems or take on your burdens, but we offer wisdom and counsel to those of you who seek to realise your full potential as divine human beings. Our mission is to remind all humanity that history will not have to repeat itself, if only enough of you take on the full responsibility of your real destiny.

The wisdom of ancestors

Many generations of human beings have lived on this planet and much of their history is unknown. In some cases, their records have been lost for all time, or may still be waiting for us to recover them from beneath the sea, within layers of growth in jungles or under ancient buildings concealed in the sand. There is very little archaeology that can guide us to 'real facts' and we must be careful not to fictionalise their lives. We can, however, glimpse these ancestors when we enter the deep layers of our collective human consciousness during meditation. Then we may ask for revelations and wise counsel; if we are prepared to open our hearts to these elders, we will be richly rewarded. Not only can we expect personal support that will help us untangle everyday issues, but we will learn how to become like the Nephalim ourselves. The human race has extraordinary potential and it should be the mission of every individual to live into their highest possibility. If not now, when?

Becoming Nephalim

By living up to our highest potential, becoming 200 per cent beings, fulfilling both our divine and our human potential, we will become Nephalim ourselves. The angelic half of our nature is waiting to be heard – what we think of as a separate Guardian Angel is really our other half. This is why we only become whole and complete when we allow our Guardian Angel to enter the blank space in our consciousness and then we feel as though we have 'come home'. This 'home' is not another place, somewhere beyond this dimension – it is here and now, waiting for us to experience it with all levels of our being. This is our divine inheritance – it cannot be taken from us, but we can neglect it and lose track of who we really are. The call of your Guardian Angel is a call to step into a new vision of what it is to be a fully realised human being. There is really no choice.

Meeting the wise ancestors

There is limited space in this book for me to help you start communicating with the Nephalim, so this is a very brief introduction (see Useful resources for details of my forthcoming book on the subject, *2012: the teachings of the Nephalim*).

When I see the Nephalim in my inner visions, I see them as ageless people – they are old, but seem very youthful. Despite their biblical names, they do not all appear to be of Middle Eastern origin, but represent a variety of racial types. The men do not always have beards but when they do, the beards are long and curling. Some of the men and women have silver hair; several of the women wear head coverings and some of the men wear turbans. I usually see them wearing flowing robes made of brightly coloured cloth – plain colours and woven stripes – although sometimes I have seen both men and women wearing trousers. I have no doubt you will see them in different ways, but their physical appearance when they were living on Earth is of no interest to us. What we are asking for is their wise counsel. On several occasions, I have noticed them carrying man-made objects, such as books, water jugs and building tools. When I noticed a dove with Noah and a lamb with Aniki, I asked if each of the other Nephalim could be associated with a creature; then I was introduced to a series of animals and birds that embody something of the *nephal* qualities. These creatures were all white. I was told that the appearance of more white creatures on our planet is a sign of changing vibrations in the Earth's aura.

Here are the twelve Nephalim that I have been communicating with, together with key words that describe the qualities they can bring in to your life:

Nephal	English name	Key words	Power animal
Seth	Appointed One	Self-mastery, commitment, choice	White lion
Azura	Lady of the High Mountains	Clarity, compassion, strength	Snow leopard
Mahaleel	Shining One	Radiance, shining beacon, star of light	White peacock
Aaliyah	Highly Exalted	Esteem, honour, reverence	Swan
Jared	The One Who Descends	Incarnation, divine man, steward	Ermine
Baraka	Bringer of Blessings	Harmony, balance, blessing	White doe
Enoch	God's Prophet	Transformation, dedication, alignment	White raven
Malkha Ora	Queen of Light	Rejuvenation, pleasure, delight	Unicorn
Methuselah	Thoughtful One	Consideration, prayer, reflection	White buffalo
Saha	Awakener	Illumination, enlightenment, realisation	Snowy owl
Noah	Comforter	Protection, loyalty, stability	Dove
Aniki	Woman of Grace	Constancy, tenderness, nourishment	Lamb

Visualisation: **The Wisdom of the Ancestors**

❖ By now, you should find it easy to take yourself to your sacred building (see p. 67), where you can sit, feeling at one with your Guardian Angel.

❖ Today you are going to ask for advice from the Nephalim – our wise ancestors – remarkable people who have lived on our planet and now dwell in the Ancestral Halls. They are not Angels, but they have lived human lives to the highest possibility and we can ask them for advice.

❖ You have already decided what you need to ask. You do not have to move from your sacred room, but you can invite the Nephalim to join you. In your heart, you ask: 'Wise Ancestors, please be present for me today, so that I can consult you about some issues in my life.'

❖ As you gaze around the room, you see several people materialising. They seem to arrive as shafts of light, then become more solid. There are men and women, and all of them are dressed in simple garments, in a variety of colours. Their complexions vary, so that it is not clear what nationality they might be.

❖ Some of the men have long hair and beards; some have short hair and smooth faces. The women's hair also varies in style and length. They seem to be timeless people, but all of them glow with a soft light that appears to radiate from every cell of their being.

❖ A semicircle of chairs appears in front of you and your visitors sit down. All except one, who is their spokesperson today – a woman in a sky-blue dress. You realise that she is Azura, Lady of the High Mountains.

❖ Now is your time to ask any questions, so I am going to leave you for a moment or two while you talk to Azura and listen to the advice from the Wise Ancestors.

(Short silence.)

❖ When you have received your answers from the Wise Ancestors, acknowledge their help and say 'thank you'. Azura bows to acknowledge you and then she joins the others as they melt away into shafts of light and disappear from sight.

❖ You sit quietly for a moment, considering what has taken place. You know that if all your questions have not yet been answered, some thoughts or dreams will arise over the next few days that will fill in the gaps.

❖ You also know that at any time you can come back to your sacred building and ask to speak to the Nephalim, who can be a source of wisdom and good advice for us all, whenever we need counselling.

(Short silence.)

❖ Now get up from your special seat and move gently to the door of your sacred space. You still feel the presence of your Guardian Angel, not as a separate being, but as a light in your heart.

❖ You walk through the woods with a light step. Everything that was difficult in your life can now be experienced in a new way, knowing, as you do, that there are spiritual helpers available to you whenever you are in need.

❖ As you come back through your garden, you can see the French windows open and you run quickly towards your sofa.

Although I only started receiving messages from the Nephalim in 2009, I realised when I started to do more inner work with them that they had originally arrived in my consciousness many years earlier.

As I began to write this book, early in 2010, I remembered a passage from a previous book I had written, a novel called *Across the Crystal Sea* about a teenage girl, Dora, whose twin sister dies. Desperate to discover where her sister Amy has 'gone', Dora sets out on a mystical quest that takes her into mysterious realms. I originally wrote this story in the mid-1970s, not long after I had experienced a major spiritual opening (described in my book, *Working with Archangels*, see Theolyn's books, p. 221). I felt as though I was accessing other realms myself – as if I myself was Dora and was being shown the realm beyond death. Dora crosses the 'crystal sea', which represents the boundary between life on Earth and the invisible realms. She travels on a shining ship, guided by a 'Navigator' (her Guardian Angel), who takes her to a beautiful island where she meets Amy and is introduced to twelve Wise Guardians.

When I reread my original typed manuscript of *Across the Crystal Sea*, I realised that the Nephalim had presented themselves to me as these 'Wise Guardians' then, nearly thirty-five years ago! I am sure if you decide to work with them too, they will bring joy and wisdom into your life.

16

Crowning the Dove

The Angels keep their ancient places
Turn but a stone, and start a wing!
'Tis ye, 'tis your estranged faces
That miss the many-splendoured thing.

FRANCIS THOMPSON

Visions in our time

During the past decade or so, many people have become more aware of angelic presences. This doesn't mean to say that the Angels were not there before. In one popular Angel book I read that the Angels have been returning to help us because we are in a time of transition. But this idea doesn't make any sense at all. If the Angels had gone away then Creation would have collapsed. Angels, and all the other celestial beings we can think of, play a fundamental part in sustaining and developing divine intention as it unfolds as a manifested creation. We may be experiencing Angels more pro-foundly and more frequently, but this is because we are ready and willing to collaborate with them. If we are seeing more Angels, it is because we are waking up. Our mental shutters are falling away because we are doing more meditation, and because we have realised that the scientific, materialistic view of the universe does not tell us the whole story about the nature of reality.

People have also reported other visions of mystical cities, wise guides, unicorns and so on. All our visions rise up in our consciousness from a collective bank of information that connects us with invisible layers of reality. Our cultural heritage plays a huge part in the way our visions present themselves. There are 'archetypes' in human consciousness that are common to us all. For example, all cultures will include a god of war in their mythology, and a goddess of love; but in monotheistic religions these 'gods' will be called Archangels and, whether 'god' or 'angel', they will have different names according to the place and time they became popular. So we are nearly always bound to experience visions that fit with our conscious or unconscious expectations. If you read books that tell you various Angels appear in certain colours, you are most likely to see them that way when you meditate. A Western mystic experiencing the power of the divine feminine is likely to 'see' the Virgin Mary, in her famous blue cloak, but it is likely that a Chinese visionary experiencing the same feminine archetype would 'see' Kuan Yin as a serene goddess. We know that each of these spiritual seekers has made contact with the same universal Mother-energy, loving and compassionate in its desire to nurture humanity.

So, in January 2009 when I had a vision of a beautiful dove, I knew I had connected with a powerful archetype that was bringing some kind of message.

The dove as a symbol of the Divine Spirit that unites us all

In Western culture, the dove is a symbol of peace, hope and spiritual gifts. When the dove returns to Noah's ark with an olive twig in her beak, Noah realises that the flood is retreating and land must

197

be close by. During the famous baptism of Jesus by John the Baptist (*Luke* 3: 21–2), a dove descends from Heaven and hovers over the head of Jesus, representing the descent of the Holy Spirit. This image has been made universally famous by Christian artists for many generations and this was the first thought that came to me: that the dove represents the Divine Spirit which creates and supports all life, and unites the vast family of humanity.

Although in earlier spiritual traditions people believed that one individual person – Jesus, the Buddha or any other saint or prophet – would be a special carrier of the Divine Spirit, I firmly believe that in this era we are seeing the Spirit working through many individuals and through large groups of people. One person will have a vision and very soon many others will say they have experienced the same or a similar vision. Modern communications technology allows us to share our visions and mystical messages rapidly, which confirms this phenomenon. We are able to compare our experiences and this, in turn, further promotes the spread of the 'good news'.

Whenever I have shared my vision of the dove, I hear similar stories and I am quite sure this means that new possibilities are showering down on us. The dove descending over Jesus heralded the advent of a new spiritual possibility for the people of his time and the generations to follow. But the image of a bird as herald is not just found in the Judeo-Christian tradition. For instance, the Mayans venerated the quetzal bird, which was associated with Quetzalcoatl, an incarnation of the Feathered Serpent deity who would descend to Earth to inspire the people. After writing the first draft of this chapter, I had a visit from my eldest daughter, who makes quilts. She showed me a new piece of fabric with a print on it, apparently of a white quetzal bird. With its beautiful long tail feathers, it looked very much like the bird I thought was a dove. The myth says that Quetzalcoatl will return as a white-bearded messenger to help humanity in times of difficulty. Perhaps the dove and the quetzal bird are both suitable signs that will draw our attention to the pressing need for a change of hearts and minds.

Because my dove vision was so dramatic, I took a note of the time: 1.30 a.m. GMT on the 12 January 2009. In astrology, the Moon's North Node represents the possibility of change and development – a new future. In the chart for my vision, the North Node was right next to Mercury – the Messenger – whose Archangel is Gabriel. On the other end of the line, at the South Node, sat the Moon, indicating that the message had come from the collective psyche. I have no doubt that many people around the world were having dreams and visions that night, all of which would have been telling a very similar story. An awakening is happening. It is not a fixed, dramatic event, but a gradual process of development, signalled by an increasing number of signs and wonders.

The crown as a symbol of enlightenment and wisdom

The dove I saw in my vision was shining; her feathers were glowing with exquisite white light, brilliant against the dark night sky. This bird was not like a painted image from some Old Master, but alive with cosmic energy. She was shaped more like a phoenix than a traditional dove and had a long tail, which moved through the sky like a comet, illuminating the night. She expanded her wings and tail, and they stretched out as luminous feathers until the sky was full of her brilliance. As the dove moved through the skies, she created a vibrating tunnel of energy – at once turbulent, but with a sense of direction, as though a portal was being created, through which I could step into an even brighter light, golden like sunshine. As I followed the dove, I noticed a glow of bright colours, like a rainbow, gathering around her head and I began to see that she was wearing a golden crown, studded with coloured gems.

Later, I realised that the dove's crown represented a new state of consciousness. In ancient times, pharaohs, popes and monarchs wore crowns to represent their divine status. They were regarded as divine emissaries on Earth. The crown circles the head, indicating that divine inspiration is available to the wearer. What I believe the crowned dove was telling me is that we are collectively moving into a different kind of awareness, which will allow us to experience our divine humanity in a way that has been lost to us. Our ancient ancestors had some success, but perhaps suffered from too much arrogance, believing that they could take charge of life on Earth without due respect for the natural order. Now we need to work hard to get it right for ourselves and future generations. If we are committed to this task and focus our whole attention in that direction, an abundance of spiritual gifts is available to us. When we accept our Guardian Angel's invitation to our own inner coronation, we will step into our true heritage and be crowned as divine human beings.

Signs and wonders herald a new future

Our human culture is going through a period of extreme turbulence. The economic 'religion' of capitalism is failing, in the same way that the Roman Catholic Church was collapsing in the fifteenth century. In those days Martin Luther famously pinned a challenge on a church door, and when we look at our newspaper and media coverage we too can see the 'writing on the wall' for the present-day hierarchy, which consists mainly of financiers and bankers. Like those ancient cultures that disappeared in previous centuries, our own civilisation is tumbling like a house of cards.

All around us there are obvious signs that old structures are falling apart, but we can also see new seeds being planted. We are being forced to tidy up our collective garden, clear out old brambles, dig out roots, redesign the landscape and plant again. Just as the invention of the printing press allowed new ideas to spread in the fifteenth century, we have the advantage of modern technology, which allows us to communicate with each other with an immediacy that we could never have imagined fifty years ago. The internet has been described as 'the enemy of the state', because people can use it to take collective power. Dreams and visions were the hallmark of the old prophets, who would then declaim the signs to the tribe. People would gather around in a market square to listen to the seer. Now we can share our visions on the worldwide web. We can pool resources and call meetings when we decide to take action. But can we step into the new responsibility that this entails?

The cinema is another place where collective dreams may be brought into our consciousness, and the movies play a huge role in sharing visions of the future. Filmmakers have the ability to influence our expectations: they can paint pictures of doom and gloom or visions of exciting new possibilities. Vast amounts of money have been spent on apocalyptic-style films that envision the destruction of great cities as an ice age descends, or as huge tidal waves engulf land that once seemed stable and secure. Are the filmmakers playing a prophetic role, warning us of dark times ahead? Or are they tapping into our unconscious fears and anxieties, and, by creating remarkable images watched by thousands of people, adding fuel to our negative thoughts? This is potentially very dangerous, because what we imagine becomes reality when our feelings generate the energy to manifest what is in our mind.

Either way, change is afoot. As the great drama of spiritual expansion for humanity is unfolding, the seas of life are bound to be choppy, but if your personal lifeboat has a reliable navigator, then you will always be in the right place at the right time. Your navigator is your Guardian Angel, your divine other half. When you have developed a truly intimate relationship with your Guardian Angel you, as the Captain, and your Guardian Angel as the Navigator, will work together as one. This will be a winning combination, that can steer your 'ship of life' towards calm seas and bright new horizons.

Can we step into our real power?

The Tree of Life from the Jewish mystical tradition describes the flow of energy as invisible possibilities, gradually manifesting as material Creation – as light descends and becomes the beauty of the tangible world. Each container (*sefira*) of light is guarded by an Archangel, but there is one point on the Tree that represents an open-ended portal, an 'empty room' that allows new potential to emerge. This space, called *Da'at* (knowledge) in Hebrew, means that the patterns of Creation are not fixed, but have room to develop and unfold.

From a spiritual perspective, this space allows us to 'think outside the box' and to develop our consciousness. Mostly, we use our brainpower to assimilate and analyse data that comes into our minds through the five senses. Because we do this all the time (except when meditating), we have a strong tendency to think of ourselves as receivers of information, moving around in a world that is already 'out there', and we learn somehow to fit into this 'real world'. We adapt ourselves to whatever seems to be going on because we have been educated to experience the world in that way, by our families and teachers. A recent popular book, *The Secret* (see Recommended books, p. 223) introduced many more people to this ancient wisdom, which teaches that we are not simply passive receivers in this world, but we are actively co-creating what is going on – whether we realise this consciously or not. There *is* an empty space when the next thing that can possibly happen has not yet happened, and how we think and behave in that moment will have an effect on what actually does happen.

At this unstable time in human history, we have the collective opportunity to choose what happens for our species. If we step into our divine possibilities, we can be reborn into a new state of con-sciousness – 'cosmic' consciousness. The crown on the dove, like the flowering of the crown *chakra* in the Indian Yogic tradition, repre-sents the highest achievement of spiritual wisdom and awareness.

In December 2012, the Earth will align with the Galactic Centre and will pass through showers of cosmic rays. It is a scientific fact that these rays can affect DNA, so the whole human race may be facing a major change. The last time this happened, about six and a half thousand years ago, coincided with the beginning of the oldest recorded civilisations. Perhaps the cosmic rays provoked a rapid evolution in our mental capacity, enabling us to develop cal-culation systems and systems of writing. There was certainly a very sudden change in human behaviour as the early hunter-gatherers began to build cities and organise societies in a completely new way. The most significant shift was from small tribal cultures to complex social structures that allowed one person, or a very small group of people, to take charge and accumulate wealth and power at the expense of the others. This process disempowered the majority in a very fundamental way – it was not just an economic issue, but also a spiritual one. Kings and pharoahs not only manipulated the material wealth in their lands, but deprived their subjects of the knowledge that would allow them to create abundance and prosperity for themselves. As this manipulation, for the benefit of the few, goes against natural law, it cannot last and, eventually, 'the last will be first and the first will be last' as Jesus put it (*Matthew* 20:16). This is what is happening to us now – it is affecting our society's top-heavy institutions and is also impacting on the ecology of the Earth. But 2012 offers us a new vision and the Guardian Angels are calling us to participate.

Divine Light in Charing Cross: how we can bring Heaven to Earth

The story of the Israelites, enslaved in Egypt and led by Moses to a 'Promised Land', reminds us that underdogs can reclaim their power. The most important thing that God gave Moses was not the famous Ten Commandments, but a description of divine creative power. God's statement, 'I am that I am', is followed by a reminder that when we are at one with the Oneness of the Divine, all things will come easily to us, without effort:

> ... great and goodly cities, which thou didst not build, and houses full of good things, which thou didst not fill, and cisterns hewn out, which thou didst not hew, and olive trees, which thou didst not plant, and thou shalt eat and be satisfied ...
>
> (*Deuteronomy* 6: 10–11)

This is the magic of co-creation! By developing our consciousness beyond the narrow focus of our personal worries and anxieties, we can step into Oneness and co-create Heaven on Earth. The energy flowing up and down Jacob's ladder will shine everywhere. We are all divine as well as human, our capacity for extending and expanding our consciousness is hard-wired into us. This state of knowledge and understanding won't actually be something new it is just that the full potential of our consciousness will be awakened. Mystics and saints throughout the centuries have received individual awakenings, but this is a collective one and we are moving towards it rapidly. The alignment in December 2012 may well provide a significant boost in a process that has already begun. It could be a crossroads at which we must decide our new direction. Are you ready and willing to be a very different kind of human being – perhaps a member of a newly evolved species? No longer *homo sapiens* but *homo angelicus*?

I hope the exercises and visualisations in this book will help you develop your relationship with your Guardian Angel so that, together, you can step into a remarkable new future with joy and with confidence.

See you there!

At once, as soon as I saw it,
The glory looked like my own self.
I saw it all in all of me,
And saw me all in all of it –
That we were twain in distinction,
And yet again in one likeness …
And my Mantle of sparkling colours
I wrapped entirely over myself.

('The Robe of Glory', Syriac Christian hymn, 2nd century)

APPENDIX 1

Meditation

Why you need to include meditation in your life, every day

Meditation is an essential process for anyone wanting to develop their spiritual gifts and maintain contact with the divine wisdom that resides within us all. Just like cleaning your teeth or taking a shower, you should make meditation a natural part of your daily routine.

Furthermore, meditation is not merely a relaxation technique designed to help you 'chill out' and escape the stress of everyday life. Yes, you will be more relaxed if you meditate regularly and events that would normally cause strong emotional reactions will just seem to be part of the flow of life. But the most important reason for meditating is that each time you withdraw from outer activities you have the opportunity to explore your inner kingdom and connect with the power of the Divine Source within. It is like plugging in to an infinite resource of energy and wisdom. Meditation promotes health and vitality, and allows you to integrate all four levels of your being – spiritual, mental, emotional and physical.

What meditation does for you

The positive effects of meditation are far-reaching. When you meditate regularly you will notice improvements in all aspects of your life. Some of the physiological effects of regular meditation have been scientifically measured, which is why medical practitioners often recommend it to their clients. Many ordinary people who take up meditation report profound changes in their personal lives, and groups of meditators report measurable results in their communities.

Physiological effects

During meditation, your blood pressure and heart rate slow down and your breathing pattern becomes slower, deeper and fuller. Sometimes, you will notice that your whole body seems to almost stop, as though you are hibernating. This stillness allows the body to heal and rebalance. The rest in meditation extends to every cell in the body and is much more profound and beneficial than sleep. You will find you need less sleep and that you are more energetic if you meditate twice a day. Physical stillness also allows you to experience deeper levels of your being and you can easily feel the presence of divine spiritual energy as it vibrates in your system. This is why people sometimes feel a vibration in their body when they meditate, as though all their cells are livening up.

Occasionally, people find themselves moving or swaying in a circular pattern while they are in deep meditation. This is because the central core of energy in our system is like a coil and meditation allows it to wind and rewind, creating powerful vibrations through all our cells. The spinning energy of the *chakras* is automatically enhanced as we gently rotate. You should not try to make this happen, but it will occasionally occur spontaneously and then you can make a note of it in your Journal.

Emotional effects

Regular meditation helps you become more confident and enhances your sense of being a whole person, not just someone who is rushing around working, with occasional emotional outbursts or distress because you feel exhausted or unappreciated. Your real sense of self-worth and value comes from knowing that you are a spiritual being, a unique and special person with your own individual destiny. Any abusive or damaging relationships will naturally fall away and any addictions that normally support your emotional wellbeing will also become less of an issue. You won't have to 'try' to give up smoking, or whatever 'drug' you use – *it* will give *you* up!

You will begin to find it easier to get through the day and things will seem to go more smoothly. Problems will appear to solve themselves. People around you will also seem to be more relaxed – this is because you will be sending out loving vibrations that put even very difficult people at ease.

Mental effects

During meditation, your brainwaves change and you easily slip into brain patterns that enhance clear thinking, intuition and creativity. Your brainwaves become 'coherent' – they begin to work together harmoniously, choosing a simpler, less hyperactive way to function.

Normally, our minds suffer from 'monkey-monkey' activity, jumping from one idea to another, attempting to cope with a thousand demands and invariably not coping well with a single one. As the mind settles down during meditation, thought processes slow down, but at the same time our capacity for inspiration increases. Think of your normal mental focus as a camera lens set to a very small aperture that you use in order to concentrate on everyday activities, such as driving, making shopping lists, talking to people and so on. During meditation, this aperture expands and, instead of feeling like an individual self, struggling to keep up with everything, you begin to feel at one with the whole universe.

Our mind is like a deep ocean and usually we are like a sailor in a little boat, bobbing up and down on the surface. Sometimes, the sea is calm; sometimes it is rough. As we turn inwards to meditate, we go deep into our own individual consciousness and, at that level, we can deal with any problems that are occurring in our lives. We can think of this process as 'deep-sea diving'. And remember, deep down in the sea we can find treasures!

Often, you will find ideas and inspirations occur that help you to deal with a personal issue that previously felt really stressful. But you can go deeper into family and ancestral consciousness, where you can help to heal issues that you have inherited or that are creating problems for living relatives. Sometimes, at this level, the spirits of dead relatives will offer themselves as guides. At an even deeper level, you may meet guides who belong to the collective consciousness – spiritual teachers, such as the Buddha or Jesus. Deeper still, you can meet with your Guardian Angels, as well as Archangels and other celestial beings. As you become experienced in meditation, you become adept at exploring these realms, and can start to make choices and request help from specific guides or Angels.

Spiritual effects

At the very bottom of our ocean of consciousness is the still, silent place where we can lose our sense of self and become united with the Divine. It is quite beautiful to stay in this stillness, sometimes losing all sense of time because we have moved from the world of clocks and timetables into the infinite bliss of Divine Compassion, Intelligence and Power. We feel united with everything that exists and our personal love is united with Universal Love.

What meditation does for humanity

For thousands of years, spiritual teachers have known that when some human beings connect with their divinity it makes it easier for others to do the same. Six hundred years before the birth of Jesus, Pythagoras founded a spiritual community in Crotona, southern Italy. He believed that a certain number of people, meditating regularly and committed to living a life focused on the highest spiritual possibilities, would create a ripple effect in collective human consciousness, allowing all humanity to evolve to its highest potential. In the seventeenth century, the English mystic, George Fox, founded the spiritual movement called the Society of Friends (popularly known as the Quakers), who gathered together for 'silent worship' – their own natural way of meditation – waiting for Spirit to speak through them. During Fox's lifetime, 10 per cent of the British population was Quaker and this had a powerful effect on British society: Quakers worked to reform slavery laws and prison conditions; they created models of good business practice, encouraging entrepreneurs to provide good-quality housing and education for workers. They became very wealthy and put their money into industrial developments that enriched the lives of people at all social levels.

More recently, in the 1960s, the Indian guru and physicist, Maharishi Mahesh Yogi, came to the West and promoted the same idea. He said that if 10 per cent of a nation's population meditated, there would be a beneficial effect on the whole country, reducing crime and increasing abundance. He set up test groups to prove that meditation could generate positive results. Advanced meditators were sent to meditate in a hotel in Beirut and it was claimed that this had an effect on the violence there. In 1980 an 'ideal village' was established in Lancashire where meditators lived together in a community and established small businesses in what had been a run-down area with a high crime rate on local council estates. The local mayor of Skelmersdale learned to meditate and gave the project his blessing. The community members meditated together in a circular building with a golden dome, where they practised advanced techniques for an hour and a half twice daily. A social survey established that after the meditators moved in the local crime rate dramatically decreased.

In the 1980s, a healing group in Brighton, England, were meditating together and focused their attention on a local 'dark' spot – a run-down Victorian fountain which attracted rowdy people, drunks and drug users. After a while, the negative activities stopped and the local council restored the fountain to its former glory. Since then, Fountain groups have sprung up in many communities around the world (see Recommended websites, p. 224).

So, your meditation is not just for your own personal spiritual development – it will have a ripple effect in the collective consciousness. If you can meditate with a group of like-minded souls, you will experience how much more powerful your divine connection becomes. A level of coherence develops that allows the group to use their collective mind power to manifest positive results for the local or global community. Creating a local group that focuses on local change is a great way to start, as this allows you all to notice the results and get feedback. It really does work. Think how pleased all those Guardian Angels will be in your area.

Individually, we have a duty to clear up our own stressful and cluttered thought patterns, just as we would tidy and clean our homes. But we also have a duty to our fellow creatures and to our planet. Just as we do our recycling and help with the cleaning in a shared house, we should contribute to the collective wellbeing by doing our bit as meditators. We wouldn't stay in a house as a guest and dodge out of the chores. For many centuries, specialist spiritual practitioners – yogis in caves, nuns and monks in monasteries and mystical retreats – have been meditating and praying constantly in order to maintain the Light for all of us. But now we *all* need to contribute – many minds make Light work!

Sometimes, students confuse 'meditation' with 'visualisation', so let me explain the difference. Meditation is designed to take you to the bottom of the ocean of consciousness where you can plug in to Divine Energy. Visualisation deliberately uses your imagination to take you on a journey through layers of consciousness – *before* you reach the bottom. This is why we use visualisations for accessing information from our Guardian Angel and other celestial beings or guides.

APPENDIX 2

Shefa Symbols

Shefa is a Hebrew word meaning 'everflow'. It is the abundance of divine power, sometimes described as 'spiritual sustenance'. In Jewish mysticism we are told that every awakening 'below' is matched by an awakening from 'above'. This means that whenever we discover our spiritual essence we automatically open ourselves to spiritual sustenance, which we can channel and use to bring increased vitality and purpose in our lives. Shefa can also be used to bring about physical changes, which is why people who channel Shefa find it easy to manifest what they need, and can work as effective healers. The inspiration for using sacred symbols to promote the flow of Shefa arrived in my life in 2000. Since then, a small but growing band of committed Shefa practitioners have been using Shefa among friends, family and clients, with inspiring results.

Shefa is a technique for awakening and aligning of the flow of divine energy. This energy is our birth-right but, invariably it is blocked because we have adopted beliefs and habits that inhibit the free flow of this life-sustaining power. Shefa is not primarily a healing technique, but healing is a natural by-product – anyone who wakes their dormant spiritual energy will find a new vitality and many physical disorders will disappear.

Shefa uses sacred symbols that vibrate with the core energy field in the human body. The symbols are vibrational reminders that open inner channels so that the 'everflow' gets flowing easily – think of a plumbing system! When we open the tap and allow Shefa to flow, we not only feel fully awake, we also accelerate our natural tendency to re-balance and heal all four layers of the human system spiritual, mental, emotional and physical. Shefa has also been used very successfully on animals and plants.

The twenty-two symbols in Shefa are based on an ancient alphabet called the *Celestial Writing* that was used by Jewish mystics. No one knows exactly how old the *Celestial Writing* is, but some people suggest it was an Angelic alphabet, used to communicate with Angels. The alphabet may have been used by Solomon who had a reputation as a wise king. In those ancient times 'wisdom' meant being skilled in astrological, magical and healing practices and magicians made talismans designed individually to help promote good health, wealth and happiness. They inscribed sigils, or symbols, on precious metals and created protective amulets that had healing properties. These ancient symbols are now being rediscovered and I find they open up channels of communication with spiritual dimensions.

Each of the Shefa symbols is named after one of the letters of the Hebrew alphabet, which is reputed to have magical potential. Each symbol also has a title, which describes its attribute (see p.214) for some examples).The symbols activate responses at a subtle level and can promote changes very rapidly, at all levels. Practitioners describe Shefa as fast and extremely powerful, but at the same time very gentle.

Learning Shefa

After a four week *Access to Shefa* course, available on line, during which students will start to use Simple Meditation (see Theolyn's CD's p.222), Shefa is taught in three stages:

Shefa One is a weekend course that qualifies the healer to practice on friends, family and non-paying clients. During this weekend, the student uses the symbols in certain clearly defined patterns, creating a self-initiation process that will promote spiritual awakening and inner healing, and which also prepares the student to work with other people.

Shefa Two requires several months (six months minimum) of practice, during which the practitioner has a mentor and home study materials to support their personal spiritual development while they work with case studies. A three-day study and practice course is a requirement. After completion, the student is qualified to practice Shefa professionally with paying clients.

The SoulSchool Diploma is a teacher-training course, spread over nine months, with several days on residential courses, plus teaching practice. Students also complete *The Angels Script Consultant's Course* in order to give them a well-rounded understanding of the power of symbols and of the role of the Archangels. The Diploma qualifies practitioners to teach to Shefa 2 level. Qualified teachers can also teach other classes based on Theolyn's books and SoulSchool materials.

Before choosing to study, you can practise using Shefa symbols on your own and this will help you decide whether you would like to learn more. See p.214 for three very useful symbols that can support you in your daily life, especially when you are feeling stressed or anxious. They work most effectively if you can find a quiet moment to take a few deep breaths and centre yourself, before introducing them as images into your mind. You can also draw them in the air with your pointing finger or with your whole hand.

Cheth	**Jod**	**Schin**
Heavenly protection	Deep peace	Loving relationships

APPENDIX 3

The Archangels of the Tree of Life

The Tree of Life describes the way Divine Energy flows through Creation in repeating patterns, based on pathways and reservoirs. Each of the ten circles on the Tree of Life represents a container of this creative energy called a *sefira*, and each *sefira* has one or two archangels as its guardian. Peter Lamborn Wilson describes the tree as 'like a rose bush on which ten measureless blossoms of light appear . . . each of the roses of light will unfold its petals and reveal a winged figure' (see Recommended books p. 223).

The table overleaf shows the qualities and objects associated with each Archangel of The Tree of Life, including the keywords, colours, gemstones, flower remedies, essential oils and planets. For more information about the Archangels of the Tree of Life, I suggest you read my book, *Working with Archangels*.

Archangel	Sefira	Keywords	Colours
Sandalphon Guardian	Kingdom	Trust, reliability, stewardship	Terracotta, golden brown, stone
Auriel Companion	Kingdom	Salvation, tender loving care, grace, mending hurts	Silver, pale blue
Gabriel Messenger	Foundation	Change, messages, spiritual growth, signs	Green, turquoise
Hanael Warrior	Victory	Energy, purpose, vitality, direction, assertiveness	All shades of red
Raphael Healer	Splendour	Harmony, healing, reconciliation, love	Pink, lilac, lavender
Michael Leader	Beauty	Courage, honour, faith, protection, commitment	Gold, sunshine yellow, red
Zadkiel Comforter	Mercy	Abundance, generosity, comfort, enthusiasm	Sapphire blue, indigo, violet
Samael Tester	Severity	Discipline, adversity, limitations, responsibility	Snow white, silver
Raziel Keeper of Mysteries	Wisdom	Revelation, insight, clarity, awakening, wisdom	Electric blue
Zaphkiel Compassionate Mother	Understanding	Compassion, freedom, peace, grace	Rose pink
Metatron The Presence	Crown	Judgement, choice, karma, commitment, obligation	Bright white light
The Shekinah Queen of Heaven	Crown	Mercy, karmic release, wholeness, blessings	Night sky blue

Gemstone	Flower remedy	Essential oil	Planet
Jasper	Gentian	Frankincense	Earth
Beryl	Chicory	Jasmine	The Moon
Emerald	Scleranthus	Cedarwood	Mercury
Sardius	Impatiens	Ginger	Mars
Amethyst	Centaury	Lavender	Venus
Carbuncle	Cerato	Angelica	The Sun
Sapphire	Agrimony	Rosemary	Jupiter
Onyx	Rock rose	Neroli	Saturn
Topaz	Vervain	Peppermint	Uranus
Ligure	Clematis	Rose	Neptune
Diamond	Mimulus	Sandalwood	Pluto
Agate	Water Violet	Chamomile	Charon (Moon of Pluto)

Useful Resources

Theolyn's courses

For up to date information about current starting dates, prices and availability, please visit www.theolyn.com.

The Academy Diploma

Theolyn's Academy runs a teacher-training and spiritual development Diploma. Participating in this twelve-month course will expand your own understanding and awareness, and you will become an effective teacher able to inspire others. The Diploma qualifies you to teach Theolyn's courses yourself.

It includes home study, close personal support from Theolyn and two residentials with your fellow Diploma students. You will also cover some of the courses listed below.

SoulSchool Courses

Courses marked with a star (*) form part of the Diploma, but you can do them, even if you don't want to become a teacher.

Access courses

Access courses are online and provide video, printed and recorded materials. The first part is free, after which you have the option to continue at your own pace.

Access to Shefa A four-part course during which you will learn to use *Simple Meditation* (see Theolyn's CD's p.222). This course introduces you to Shefa and will help you decide whether you would like to proceed to Shefa One.

Access to Wisdom A nine-part course offering a taste of Theolyn's work, including Guardian Angels, Archangels, Shefa, the Nephalim and more.

eClasses

These nine-week internet classes are all based on books by Theolyn. They start in January, April and September each year. They include weekly video seminars designed to address your questions; recorded guided visualisations; printed materials; access to exclusive online discussion boards where you can share meet and share with your fellow eClassmates and Theolyn.

Your Guardian Angel needs you! Discover how to get in touch with your Divine mentor, whose awesome power will bring you a new sense of purpose, rooted in your true heart's desire.

Working with Archangels A transformative journey to meet the Archangels of the Tree of Life who will help you create a life that you love.

2012: The teaching of the Nephalim Learn how to access the practical wisdom of our semi-divine ancestors for yourself to help you manifest your heart's desire.

Angel Wisdom

These certificated courses include printed course materials, recorded guided visualisations and personal telephone support. They are available by post or online.

Module One – Living with Angels* This three-part home study course lays the foundations of a clear understanding and rapport with the angelic kingdom. It is based on Theolyn's book, *Living with Angels*, and familiarises you with the wisdom within *The Angels Script* messages.

Module Two – Messages of the Archangels* This four-part home study course is an in-depth journey with the Archangels and sacred symbols found in *The Angels Script*. It is a powerful spiritual development course that will also qualify you as an Angels Script Consultant.

Shefa

Shefa One* is a three-day hands-on workshop that qualifies you to practice Shefa on friends, family and non-paying clients. During course, you will learn how to use the symbols in certain clearly defined patterns. This will be a self-initiation process that promotes spiritual awakening and inner healing for you, and prepares you to work with other people.

Shefa Two* is a four-day hands-on workshop, followed by a minimum of six months practice, during which you will be working on case studies. You will also have a personal mentor and home study materials to support your spiritual development. After completion, you will be qualified to practice Shefa professionally on paying clients. Shefa is recognised by insurance companies.

Theolyn's books

Living with Angels, Piatkus, 2003
The Angels Script (2nd edition), SoulSchool Publishing, 2004
Working with Your Guardian Angel, Piatkus, 2005
Working with Archangels, Piatkus, 2007
2012: the teachings of the Nephalim, O Books, 2011

Theolyn's CDs

All these CDs are read by Theolyn. They are also available for download as MP3s to play on your computer or MP3 player.

Living with Angels: CD containing all the visualisations from the book.

Working with Archangels: two-CD set containing all the guided visualisations from the book.

Meeting Archangels: two-CD set of visualisations for all the Archangels of the Tree of Life.

Your Guardian Angel Needs You!: two-CD set of visualisations from the book.

2012: the teachings of the Nephalim: two-CD set containing all the visualisations from the book.

Simple Meditation: all you need to know to start using this simple but powerful mantra meditation technique. Essential practice, whatever your lifestyle, bringing reduced stress, better health and enhanced mental and spiritual abilities.

Theolyn's websites

www.theolyn.com: for information about all of Theolyn's books, CDs, courses, workshops and other activities. Also hosts Theolyn's blog.

The Angels Script Circle

This is an internet-based club for users of *The Angels Script*. For a small annual subscription, you have access to a growing library of extra materials, including teaching videos, audio downloads and printed materials. In addition, you have access to exclusive discussion boards, so you can share ideas and learn from others who use the *Script*, including Theolyn, who looks in from time to time. Visit www.theolyn.com.

Recommended books

Anderson, Joan Wester, *Guardian Angels*, Loyola University Press, 2006

Arden, Paul, *It's Not How Good You Are, It's How Good You Want to Be*, Phaidon, 2003

Astell, Chrissie, *Gifts from the Angels*, Watkins Books, 2011

Barker, Margaret, *An Extraordinary Gathering of Angels*, MQ Publications, 2004

Beck, Martha, *Finding Your Own North Star*, Piatkus, 2003

Byrne, Rhonda, *The Secret*, Simon & Schuster, 2006

Carson, David and Sams, Jamie, *Medicine Cards*, St Martin's Press, 1999

Chopra, Deepak, *Ageless Body, Timeless Mind*, Rider & Co., 2008

Crombie, Robert Ogilvie, *Gentleman and the Faun: Encounters with Pan and the Elemental Kingdom*, Findhorn Press Ltd, 2009

Davidson, Gustav, *A Dictionary of Angels*, Simon & Schuster, 1994

Dawood, N. J. (trans.), *The Koran*, Penguin Classics, 1974

Fiennes, Ralph, *Scott*, Coronet, 2004

Findhorn Community, *The Findhorn Garden Story*, Findhorn Press, 2009

Ford, Debbie, *The Secret of the Shadow*, Harper San Francisco, 2002

Guiley, Rosemary Ellen, *Angels of Mercy*, Pocket Books, 1994

Hickman, Tom, *Churchill's Bodyguard*, Headline 2006

Hicks, Esther and Jerry, *Ask and It Is Given*, Hay House, 2005

Hill, Napoleon, *Think and Grow Rich*, Wilder Publications, 2008

Iyer, Raghavan (ed.), *The Golden Verses of Pythagoras*, Concord Grove Press, 1983

Jarow, Rick, *Creating the Work You Love*, Bear & Co., 1996

Katie, Byron, *Loving What Is*, Rider & Co., 2002

Kipling, Rudyard, *Just So Stories* (specifically, 'The Elephant's Child'). There are many editions; I recommend you find one that includes Kipling's own illustrations, if you can. I suggest you also read *Old Man Kangaroo*, a cautionary tale that illustrates two wise maxims: 'Be careful what you ask for' and, 'When it comes to self-transformation, don't expect magic to be a replacement for work.'

Margolies, Morris B., *A Gathering of Angels*, Jason Aronson, 1999

Moody, Raymond, *Life after Life*, Harper San Francisco, 2001

Mohr, Barbara, *The Cosmic Ordering* Service, Hodder Mobius, 2006

Nani, Christel, *Sacred Choices*, Harmony Books, 2006

O'Brien, Christian and Barbara, *The Shining Ones*, Golden Age Project, 2001

Pepper, Kathleen, *Hand in Hand with Angels*, Polair Publishing, 2010

Sheldrake, Rupert, *A New Science of Life*, Icon Books Ltd, 2009

Sounes, Howard, *Down the Highway – the life of Bob Dylan*, Black Swan, 2002

Tolle, Eckhart, *The Power of Now*, Mobius, 2001

Wilson, Peter Lamburn, *Angels*, Thames and Hudson, 1980

Recommended websites

Joan Wester Anderson – www.joanwanderson.com

Chrissie Astell – www.angellight.co.uk

Veronique Cliquet's website, which shows the magical place where I saw a fairy (mentioned on p. 173) – www.reiki-courses-wales.co.uk

The College of Psychic Studies, established 1884 in London, offers spiritual and psychic courses to a very high standard – www.collegeofpsychicstudies.co.uk

Lauren D'Silva – www.bellaonline.com/articles/art31900.asp

The Findhorn Community – www.findhorn.org

The Golden Age Project, which collects research into the origins of human civilisation – www.goldenageproject.org.uk

Rosemary Ellen Guiley – www.visionaryliving.com

Judy Hall, an excellent astrologer – www.judyhall.co.uk

Alister Hardy Research Centre for research into spiritual and near-death experiences – http://www.lamp.ac.uk/aht/

The Isle of Avalon Foundation, which provides courses,

workshops and conferences in Glastonbury, UK –
www.isleofavalonfoundation.com
Mayan predictions for 2012, mentioned on p. 27 –
www.december212012.com/articles/disaster/4.htm
Newbold House, which is associated with Findhorn, and offers
retreats and workshops – www.newboldhouse.org
Kathleen Pepper – www.keystolight.co.uk

Index

Abulafia 55
accidents 21–3
Across the Crystal Sea 195
addictions 91, 207
Africa, West 5
Aimee's story 19–20
Air 149, 151, 166, 167, 169
alchemy 154
Alice's story 19
Alister Hardy Research Center xxii, 23
alphabets, magical 211–12
ancestors 8, 9, 93, 165, 200, 208
    Nephalim as 190, 191–5
    spirits of 168, 169, 170, 171
Anderson, Joan Wester 18–19
Angel of Death 91
angels 63–4, 93, 167–8, 196–7
    'fallen' 187–9
    requesting help from 174–6
    singing 74, 79, 104, 167, 182
    see also Archangels; Guardian Angels
Angels Script, The 78, 186, 212, 220
anger 133–4
Aniki 191, 192
anima mundi 169
animals
    four faces of Cherubim 169
    group consciousness 138–9
    negative associations 156
    Nephalim linked with 191–2
    power animals 8, 93, 169, 170, 171

Shefa healing for 211
anxiety 120, 155
apocryphal texts 16, 187, 188
appearance, visual 65, 66, 71–4
Aquinas, St Thomas 5
Archangels 6, 93, 137, 165, 167, 168, 176–9, 197, 201, 208
    Hall of 182
    names xx–xxi, 176, 177, 178, 214
    on Tree of Life xx–xxii, 177–8, 214–15
archetypes 197
Arden, Paul
    It's Not How Good You Are, It's How Good You Want To Be 108
artists 64, 156
Ascended Masters 172
ascension 149, 152
Assyrians 3–4
Astarte xix
Astell, Chrissie 11–13, 34
astrology 71, 82, 149, 169, 199, 211
Atropos 4, 43
aum 56
Auriel 178–9
Azura 192, 193

Bala'am 15–16
Balak, King of Moab 15
Basil, St 5
Bath Abbey 93
Beloved, role of 11–13
bene elohim 186–7